ESPECIALLY FOR

....

FROM

....

DATE

....

SMART START DEVOTIONS FOR YOUNG MEN

DAVID SANFORD

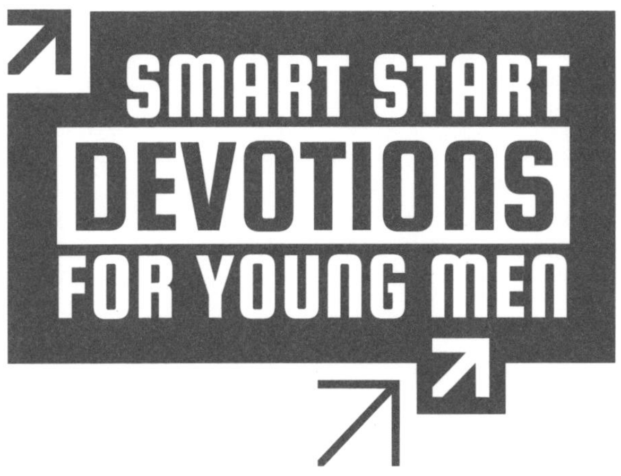

WISDOM + INSPIRATION *for* NAVIGATING ADULTHOOD—
28 WEEKS *of* READINGS PLUS INTERACTIVE "LIFE MAPS"

Previously released as *The Life Map Devotional for Men*

ISBN 979-8-89151-042-5

Cover Design: Greg Jackson, Thinkpen Design

Published by Barbour Publishing, Inc., 1810 Barbour Drive, Uhrichsville, Ohio 44683, www.barbourbooks.com.

Our mission is to inspire the world with the life-changing message of the Bible.

Printed in China.

INTRODUCTION

Business leaders say, "Plan your work, work your plan." Why not apply that idea to your whole life? After all, "The noble make noble plans, and by noble deeds they stand" (Isaiah 32:8 NIV). *Smart Start Devotions for Young Men* offers applied biblical wisdom so you can become more of the man God wants you to be.

This book features twenty-eight weekly themed introductions plus related devotional readings for five days a week (Monday through Friday). It also features two-page "life map" spreads that you can fill out to help you with that week's focused devotional time. Through the 140 entries and their accompanying life maps, you'll be encouraged to improve your knowledge of the faith, your prayer and Bible time, your finances, job, health and wellness, and more.

Smart Start Devotions for Young Men will guide you into a more intentional life—one that honors God and benefits you and others for all time to come.

Why not make this your best year ever? Make noble plans, do noble deeds, and succeed in every major area of life.

Whatever you do, work heartily, as for the Lord and not for men, knowing that from the Lord you will receive the inheritance as your reward. You are serving the Lord Christ.

COLOSSIANS 3:23–24 ESV

WEEK 1

FAITH BASICS

My dad handed me my first life map. He said, "David, there are no rules. Don't obey anyone. Don't even obey me." Pretty crazy, huh? Yes, I got hurt. Worse, I hurt others.

By age thirteen, I didn't need anyone to teach me that "all have sinned" (Romans 3:23 NIV). I needed to meet the Lord and Savior who created me, loved me, died for my sins, rose again. . .and asked me to follow Him wholeheartedly for the rest of my life. I said, "Yes!" And I've been saying yes almost every day since.

Think of this book as the opposite of *my* first life map. In these pages, I've sought to impart applied wisdom day after day. We'll start with Faith Basics for two weeks. Then we'll cover prayer, the Bible, fellowship, family, hospitality, God's will, work, rest, recreation, entertainment, personal improvement, fitness, travel, finances, giving back, and goal setting for a week or two each. We'll end with one final week focused on who God is in our lives.

I hope you resonate with these Smart Start devotions at every turn. Enjoy the adventure!

Now faith is confidence in what we hope for and assurance about what we do not see.

HEBREWS 11:1 NIV

MONDAY

THE CREATOR AND HIS CREATION

By faith we understand that the universe was formed at God's command, so that what is seen was not made out of what was visible.
HEBREWS 11:3 NIV

After I said "Yes!" to God, I realized I had a lot to learn—and I started reading the Bible. No one explained that I could read three chapters a day and finish the whole Bible in a year. So I started reading the Bible like any other book, completing it in as little as twenty-seven days.

Read the Bible like that, and you soon discover that God likes to call Himself "the Lord God, creator of heaven and earth." He could simply speak and create the whole universe. It changed how I saw God (wow!) and how I viewed creation's greatest hits (awesome!).

To be clear, I worship the Creator, not His creation. . .or any of man's creations, for that matter. Feelings of transcendence rightly have only one place to go—*up,* in worship of the God who made this all possible.

Lord, I thank You for who You are and for all You have made. Sometimes the vistas here on earth take my breath away. The night sky provokes even more awe. All because of You!

TUESDAY

GOD'S LIFE BREATHED INTO MAN

Then the Lord God formed a man from the dust of the ground and breathed into his nostrils the breath of life, and the man became a living being.

Genesis 2:7 niv

The Lord God, creator of heaven and earth, wasn't finished until He formed Adam from the dust and Eve from Adam's side. God's life was breathed into humanity and its offspring.

No wonder scripture teaches that life is a gift from God—a gift to be cherished and treasured. True, this life is only a small taste of the eternal life to come, but let's make it count!

How do we do that? The best way is to wholeheartedly desire the forever-life with God in His new heavens and new earth (Revelation 21).

That changes how I see life now, here, today. My dad was wrong: I'm not just an "accidental concatenation of molecules," to quote the Australian natural history professor Paul Davies. God's life has been breathed into me. I'm a living soul and my destiny is eternal.

Who God is makes all the difference about *who I am*. The same is true about you!

Lord, I thank You for who You are and for breathing Your life into me. You designed me to know, love, serve, and enjoy You forever. I'm happy to do so!

WEDNESDAY

GOD APPEARS TO MAN

"For God so loved the world that he gave his one and only Son [Jesus Christ], that whoever believes in him shall not perish but have eternal life."
JOHN 3:16 NIV

God loves the earth and everything He made, including you and me. No wonder then that God enjoyed appearing daily to walk with Adam and Eve in the cool of the evening.

Throughout the Old Testament (the Hebrew Bible), God kept visiting the earth. Sometimes He appeared in human- or angel-like form—what theologians call theophanies. But God can appear in any form He wishes, including storms and whirlwinds. He has even appeared as light and fire.

The New Testament describes God's ultimate visit to earth in the form of His Son, Jesus Christ. The Gospels—Matthew, Mark, Luke, and John—tell us about Jesus' life, ministry, teaching, miracles, betrayal, death, burial, and resurrection. The book of Acts describes the church's miraculous birth, expansion, gospel message, and blessed hope. The rest of the Bible offers many other important teachings.

Ultimately, the Bible tells us about Jesus Christ's second coming. I can't wait to be embraced by the Lord and actually walk with Him physically. How about you?

Lord, thank You for appearing on earth so often and at such great cost to Your Son. I'm gladly called His follower.

THURSDAY

MAN'S FALL INTO EVIL

But you, man of God, flee from all this [evil],
and pursue righteousness, godliness,
faith, love, endurance and gentleness.
1 Timothy 6:11 niv

God stopped walking with Adam and Eve the day they cooled their love and worship for Him. We may be tempted to shake our heads and wonder, "How could they?" But let's not forget our own propensity to cool off toward God.

Actually, "cool off" is an understatement. Adam and Eve decided the serpent—God's enemy, Satan, the devil—was telling the truth when he said God was holding out on them. So the first couple decided to take things into their own hands. They walked out of God's will and into the deadly way of the enemy of their (and *our*) souls. Though they were sent out of the Garden of Eden, God had a rescue plan for them and everyone to follow.

On this earth, Satan wants to steal from, kill, and destroy unsuspecting men. The devil often does this with a truth, a half-truth, and a lie (see his approach in Genesis 3:1–4). It's deadly serious business.

Lord, thank You for rescuing Adam and Eve and sending
Your Son, Jesus Christ, to die for me and my sins.
Help me to see through Satan's every ploy to ruin my life.

FRIDAY

TIME AND ETERNITY

Fight the good fight of the faith. Take hold of the eternal life to which you were called when you made your good confession in the presence of many witnesses.
1 TIMOTHY 6:12 NIV

God doesn't give us a thousand-dollar gold coin every time we say "Yes!" to His Word, His will, and His ways. No, He has something far more valuable reserved for us in heaven. We know this from the words of Jesus, yet do we hold these promises close to our heart? Sometimes. Sometimes not.

Mathematically, *infinity* and *eternity* eclipse seventy-five trillion dollars and a hundred billion years. And it's not even close. To understand this is paramount to living wisely in our finite, time-bound world. No wonder the apostle Paul calls us to "fight the good fight of the faith" and "take hold of the eternal life to which you were called."

During this weekend, be sure to complete the first of the twenty-eight life maps in this book. Completing them is the key to mining the full benefit from this adventure. Enjoy!

Lord, thank You for the Faith Basics I've covered this week. Show me ways each idea applies to me at this stage of my life. Please bless me, Lord, I pray.

Lord, this week we've considered powerful truths that appear in the opening pages of scripture and that reverberate through the rest of the Bible—most of all, how great You are!

5 TOPICS COVERED THIS WEEK:

MONDAY: the Creator and His creation
TUESDAY: God's life breathed into man
WEDNESDAY: God appears to man
THURSDAY: man's fall into evil
FRIDAY: time and eternity

3 WAYS GOD'S CREATION WOWS ME:

1 ....

2 ....

3 ....

3 WAYS MAN'S FALL HAUNTS ME:

1 ....

2 ....

3 ....

How I want to respond to these truths:

....

....

....

....

....

....

....

LORD, HERE'S WHAT'S GOING ON IN MY LIFE RIGHT NOW. . .

OTHER THINGS I NEED TO SHARE WITH YOU, LORD. . .

Lord, when it comes to this new life map, I need to. . .

Without faith it is impossible to please God, because anyone who comes to him must believe that he exists and that he rewards those who earnestly seek him.

HEBREWS 11:6 NIV

Thank You, Lord, for hearing my prayers and for helping me take action!

AMEN.

WEEK 2

MORE FAITH BASICS

The first week we considered the Faith Basics of the Creator and creation, of God's life breathed into man, of the Lord's appearances to man, of man's fall into evil, and of the vast and weighty difference between time and eternity.

This second week—before we begin considering each major sphere of life for six months—we have five more Faith Basics to cover. We will consider our Lord Jesus Christ, our faith's good works, the certainty of God's judgment, knowing what's true and what's not, and going deeper into God's Word, the Bible.

The more we learn from God's Word (and the more we trust the Lord Himself), the more we will enjoy His good hand of blessing in our lives. Not the "everything goes my way" kind of blessings, but the true gifts of peace with God and others, belonging and significance, hope for the future, and much, much more.

May your sense of forgiveness and belonging increase this week!

"Receive forgiveness of sins and a place among those who are sanctified by faith in me [Jesus Christ]."

ACTS 26:18 NIV

MONDAY

OUR LORD JESUS CHRIST

Through [Jesus Christ] you believe in God,
who raised him from the dead and glorified him,
and so your faith and hope are in God.
1 PETER 1:21 NIV

Certain decisions you make can change the whole trajectory of your life. Good choices can produce more positive results than you could possibly imagine from the outset. First is the decision to become a wholehearted follower of Jesus Christ.

It's not enough to believe Jesus was God with us. It's not enough to know He died for our sins on a Roman cross, was buried, and rose again from the grave three days later. *Knowing* is only the starting point. The Lord calls us to consciously, actively, and deeply put our belief, faith, trust, hope, and love in God.

There was a day in my life when I *knew* I loved Renée—I wanted to marry her, and I couldn't imagine the rest of my life without her. Similarly, we should never imagine our lives without Jesus at the forefront. Because He reigns supreme over heaven and earth, we will gladly follow the Lord each day.

Lord, thank You for bringing me to faith in You and
changing the whole trajectory of my life—here on earth
and for eternity. I can't imagine my life without You.

TUESDAY

OUR FAITH'S GOOD WORKS

We keep on praying for you, asking our God to enable you to live a life worthy of his call. May he give you the power to accomplish all the good things your faith prompts you to do.
2 Thessalonians 1:11 NLT

When I finally admitted what my heart told me—and realized I couldn't imagine my life without Renée—my thoughts, words, and actions changed. I couldn't wait to travel to her place, spend hours with her in person, and then spend still more hours on the phone and writing letters until we could see each other again.

In every way, I wanted to please Renée, to demonstrate that I was worthy of her love and affection. I didn't just daydream, but spent real time and money on travel, gifts, and dining. And I wanted to do ever more.

Similarly, Renée and I want to do ever more for the Lord, even after all these years. The secret? God's power is in us, prompting us to do more for Him. That is, more good works for His glory, honor, and praise. May that be your desire too!

Lord, I want to do ever more for You. Thank You for Your power at work in and through me. Please prompt me to do something more for You today.

WEDNESDAY

THE CERTAINTY OF GOD'S JUDGMENT

It is appointed for man to die once,
and after that comes judgment.
HEBREWS 9:27 ESV

I deeply feared telling Renée that I loved her. Any response less than "I love you too!" would have devastated my heart. On the other hand, two years later I had absolutely no fear of asking Renée to marry me. True, any response less than jumping into my arms and breathlessly saying "Yes!" would have killed me. Still, I had no fear. The difference? Knowing that Renée *already* had judged me worthy of her lifelong love and affection.

One of Satan's biggest lies questions whether or not we can trust God. Another big lie questions how God operates. He's not a tired old man slowly reading a book about us, then looking up and wondering what judgment to render. What a terrible misrepresentation of God!

When we appear before Him someday, His judgments will be sure. He knows everything (Psalm 147:5)! On that day, the Lord won't be rolling the dice. What He announces will be true, right, and good.

Lord, I thank You that I can trust You fully—
especially what You will do and say on judgment day.
I know I am covered by Jesus' sacrifice. Amen!

THURSDAY

WHAT'S TRUE AND WHAT'S NOT

We demolish arguments and every pretension that sets itself up against the knowledge of God, and we take captive every thought to make it obedient to Christ.
2 Corinthians 10:5 NIV

The devil knows a lot of languages, but only one way to speak. And not just a lie here and there, but a rushing torrent of flaming darts designed to knock us off our feet. We fight back in two ways.

First, we identify Satan's lies and demolish them with God's truth. Then we carefully examine every new thought that comes our way. Our key question: Does this thought accurately reflect Jesus Christ and align with God's Word?

Secondly, we let our minds be transformed in keeping with the verse above, as well as with Romans 12:1–2 and other scriptures.

The enemy never tires of attacking our hearts and minds, so we must always be alert. But we can be confident that God's truth and justice will always prevail.

Lord, give me strength to keep fighting Satan's lies and test every new thought that comes my way. Speak to me, lead me, guide me. Keep me fighting the good fight, I pray.

FRIDAY

GOD'S WORD, THE BIBLE

All Scripture is breathed out by God and profitable for teaching, for reproof, for correction, and for training in righteousness, that the man of God may be complete, equipped for every good work.
2 Timothy 3:16–17 ESV

Shortly after Renée and I started dating, we supplemented visits and weekend phone calls with lots of full-length letters every week. Every day or two I was walking on the clouds. Then the letters from Renée stopped. After three letterless days, I had crashed to earth. By day four, I was depressed out of my mind.

Soon, I had resigned myself to serving God as a single missionary. . .and dying young. But then they appeared: six letters from Renée, written on six different days, but all delivered by the postal service at the same time. *Yes! My life goes on!*

Thankfully, God's letters to us—the books of the Bible—are all available, all the time. His Word tells us everything we need to know for life and good works.

If you want more zest out of life, quit searching elsewhere. . .dive deeper into God's holy and inspired Word. It's brought such tremendous power, joy, and peace into my life—it can do the same in yours!

Lord, thanks for giving us Your Word. I want to learn it better in the weeks and years to come.

DATE: ....

Lord, how wonderful that I need not worry whether I should trust You. You have promised and shown a deep, deep love for me. You are righteous in all You say and do!

5 TOPICS COVERED THIS WEEK:

MONDAY: our Lord Jesus Christ
TUESDAY: our faith's good works
WEDNESDAY: the certainty of God's judgment
THURSDAY: what's true and what's not
FRIDAY: God's Word, the Bible

3 WAYS GOD'S LOVE INSPIRES ME:

1 ....

2 ....

3 ....

3 WAYS SATAN'S LIES HAVE TRIPPED ME UP:

1 ....

2 ....

3 ....

How I want to respond to these truths:

....

....

....

....

....

....

....

....

LORD, HERE'S WHAT'S GOING ON IN MY LIFE RIGHT NOW. . .

OTHER THINGS I NEED TO SHARE WITH YOU, LORD. . .

Lord, when it comes to this new life map, I need to. . .

In the gospel the righteousness of God is revealed—a righteousness that is by faith from first to last, just as it is written: "The righteous will live by faith."

ROMANS 1:17 NIV

Thank You, Lord, for hearing my prayers and for helping me take action!

AMEN.

WEEK 3

PRAYING FOR YOURSELF

Does it seem selfish to pray for yourself? You and I may choose to pray often for others (which is great!) but feel less comfortable talking to God about our own needs. But that is appropriate prayer too.

God repeatedly invites us to ask Him for things we need. Jesus asked people, "What do you want me to do for you?" In fact, *not* asking is wrong. God was angry with King Ahab when he refused to ask for anything (Isaiah 7:10–14). When King Asa refused to pray about his own serious illness, he died (2 Chronicles 16:12). In both cases, their blatant unwillingness to pray revealed a lack of love for God and failure to trust Him.

Yes, we will experience God's power answering our prayers for other people, but He also wants us to experience His power to answer *our* prayers, meet *our* needs, and change *our* lives.

This week we will take time to ponder what it means to pray for ourselves—and do it!

"What do you want me to do for you?" Jesus asked him. The blind man said, "Rabbi, I want to see."

MARK 10:51 NIV

MONDAY

EXPERIENCE YOURSELF AS GOD DOES

"The Father himself loves you dearly because you love me and believe that I came from God."
John 16:27 NLT

When I come to the Lord to pray for myself, I must first experience myself as He does. Do I imagine God hears me as a bothersome interruption or an unwelcome visitor? If so, I will hesitate to go to God with my needs, my hurts, and my deepest desires. Then again, if I know that I am God's beloved child, I'll trust He hears my voice with delight. He says, "Pull up a chair! I was waiting for you. I want to hear everything!"

When I pray for myself, I begin by thanking God for who He is and who He made me to be. I don't ask for anything, I just rejoice—as any man does when he experiences God's deep love. Like a child looking up to his father, I fix my eyes on Jesus. . .and His love draws me closer to His heart.

If you haven't experienced yourself as God does, ask Him to make this your reality. It's a prayer He delights to answer!

Lord, before anything else, I want to know and experience who I am to You. Then I can enjoy Your love for me.

TUESDAY

BARE YOUR SOUL

I cry out to the Lord; I plead for the Lord's mercy. I pour out my complaints before him and tell him all my troubles.

Psalm 142:1–2 NLT

When I pray for myself, I can bare my soul completely to God. God can handle any emotions I'm experiencing and any questions I bring. He isn't uneasy or afraid or caught off guard.

In the Bible, David constantly poured out his frustrations, anger, sorrow, and longings to God—and we read them today as the psalms. David's strong words may make us feel uncomfortable, but their place in scripture proves that we too can be completely honest with God. We can rant and rave and ask any question—though, like Job, we may be stunned by God's direct answers.

Moses certainly complained while talking with the Lord. Nehemiah prayed his heart out for four months asking God to restore the city of Jerusalem. Paul begged God deeply on three occasions to remove a painful "thorn" in his life.

God already knows our hearts, but He wants to hear our cries. He also wants to hear our trust in Him. No one but God can be trusted to understand and rescue us.

Lord, I open my heart to You—no hiding, no pretending. I know that I can trust You completely.

WEDNESDAY

INVITE GOD'S WORK IN YOUR LIFE

Search me, God, and know my heart; test me and know my anxious thoughts. See if there is any offensive way in me, and lead me in the way everlasting.

PSALM 139:23–24 NIV

As my Maker, God knows me fully and intimately. He understands me more completely than I will ever understand myself. As human beings, we only know ourselves in a very limited fashion—I don't know most of my own motives and faults, or I easily overlook them. When I come to God, I need to slow down.

Praying for myself starts best with introspection. I ask God not only to forgive me for my daily sins, but also for the patterns of disobedience, unkindness, or selfishness in my life. I ask the Holy Spirit to reveal these to me and to change me from the inside out. When the Spirit answers, His voice will be one of conviction about specific sin or needed change—not the enemy's lies that say I'm hopeless and I'll never be forgiven.

The answer to my prayers for myself is *God*—our unique Lord who can bring about the change (the "spiritual fruit") that comes from following Him.

Lord, show me who I am and where I need to change. Then bring growth in my life that makes me more like Jesus.

THURSDAY

PRAY WHEN ANXIOUS AND DEPRESSED

Enter his gates with thanksgiving, and his courts with praise! Give thanks to him; bless his name!
Psalm 100:4 esv

How often have you lain awake at night, your mind swirling with anxiety and your spirit crushed with depression? Perhaps you cry out to the Lord in prayer, but the thoughts keep coming—you can't turn them off. The morning may bring sunshine, but you wear a heavy jacket of worry all day. How do you pray when your spirit is dark—and God hasn't promised an easy fix?

During such times, two guardrails have kept me centered on the highway of prayer: thankfulness and God's Word. When I'm awake and my thoughts won't stop, I fill my mind with worship for who God is and thankfulness for what He's done. And when a troubling situation or person comes to mind, I have a verse ready to recite. To name two favorites: "Rejoice in the Lord always; again I will say, rejoice" (Philippians 4:4 esv) or "Don't worry about anything; instead, pray about everything" (Philippians 4:6 nlt).

Worship settles my mind and fills my spirit. Scripture brings new joy and life to my soul.

Lord, I will fill my mind with thoughts of You and Your Word. . .and You will give me life.

FRIDAY

MAKE REQUESTS

"Then you will know that I am the LORD;
those who hope in me will not be disappointed."
ISAIAH 49:23 NIV

You've walked through God's gates with thanksgiving. You've prayed for the Lord to search your heart. You've asked Him to change you from the inside out.

What else is on your heart and mind? Ask the Lord to respond to each concern in a specific, detailed manner. Then watch for His answers. Don't rush by and miss them! When we experience God's specific replies to our prayers, our faith and trust deepen.

For many years, I hesitated to ask God for specific personal needs—I didn't want to put Him in the position of disappointing me. In time, though, I learned that God's "no" was also an answer, one that meant He would give me something better. I began to look for the "other" answers He was giving me instead.

When praying for yourself, find and quote a scripture or two. That way, you'll have the right words to express your needs and desires. You'll know you are praying in God's will, and the very words you pray will change and strengthen you.

Lord, please show me Your goodness and power by answering my prayers for my own needs. Increase my faith as I see Your good work in my life.

Lord, thank You for making me Your beloved child. I'm so glad You hear my voice with delight and say, "Pull up a chair! I was waiting for you. I want to hear everything!"

5 TOPICS COVERED THIS WEEK:

MONDAY: experience yourself as God does
TUESDAY: bare your soul
WEDNESDAY: invite God's work in your life
THURSDAY: pray when anxious and depressed
FRIDAY: make requests

3 WAYS PRAYING PERSONALLY CHANGES ME:

1 ....

2 ....

3 ....

3 WAYS PRAYING SPECIFICALLY CONCERNS ME:

1 ....

2 ....

3 ....

How I want to respond to these truths:

....

....

....

....

....

....

....

....

LORD, HERE'S WHAT'S GOING ON IN MY LIFE RIGHT NOW. . .

OTHER THINGS I NEED TO SHARE WITH YOU, LORD. . .

Lord, when it comes to this new life map, I need to. . .

"Ask and it will be given to you; seek and you will find; knock and the door will be opened to you."
MATTHEW 7:7 NIV

Thank You, Lord, for hearing my prayers and for helping me take action!
AMEN.

WEEK 4

PRAYING FOR OTHERS

When you pray for others, how do you feel? Bored? Thrilled? Somewhere in between?

One time, after a seminar I'd led, a woman walked up to me to say she was suffering greatly from stage 4 ovarian cancer. Had I been in a church, I would have gathered other believers, anointed this lady with a few drops of olive oil, and prayed for her healing. I didn't have the opportunity to do that at the seminar, but I did what I could. With tear-filled eyes, I put my hand on Valerie's shoulder and pleaded with the Lord to heal her.

It's always a humbling thing to pray for a person's physical healing. We're saying, "We're absolutely dependent on You, Lord." Sometimes (praise God) people are healed here and now. . .sometimes they die and go to glory. Either way, I feel helpless, reliant on God and God alone.

Then again, complete dependence on God is what we *should* feel every time we pray for ourselves and others. (And complete gratitude when God says "yes" to our earnest, heartfelt prayers, as He did for Valerie just seven weeks later!)

For all of God's promises have been fulfilled
in Christ with a resounding "Yes!"
2 CORINTHIANS 1:20 NLT

MONDAY

PRAY FOR YOUR CHRISTIAN FRIENDS

We always thank God, the Father of our Lord Jesus Christ, when we pray for you, because we have heard of your faith in Christ Jesus and of the love you have for all God's people.

COLOSSIANS 1:3–4 NIV

When you pray for your Christian friends, what do you think and know and believe? Do you expect God to answer your prayers in specific, detailed ways? Do you thank the Lord for making your friends trophies of His love, mercy, and grace? Okay, *trophies* probably isn't the word you would use, but you get the idea.

Besides praying specifically and thankfully, I always try to reflect on God's marvelous, amazing mercy and grace. This requires that I extend instant, full, unconditional mercy and grace to the people who wound or hurt me. Doing this releases new blessings in my own life.

Those blessings include the experience (and overflow) of God's love in and through me. After all, "What is important is faith expressing itself in love" (Galatians 5:6 NLT). May that love inspire your prayers for your friends.

Lord, I thank You for all the prayers that others have lifted up on my behalf through the years. I want to pray more often for them.

TUESDAY

PRAY FOR YOUR CHRISTIAN COLLEAGUES

With this in mind, we constantly pray for you, that our God may make you worthy of his calling, and that by his power he may bring to fruition your every desire for goodness and your every deed prompted by faith.

2 THESSALONIANS 1:11 NIV

I always smile when a friend tells me that he's the only Christian at his workplace. "How many people work at your company?" I ask. If it's more than ten or fifteen, I challenge the assertion.

First, I say, assume that at least one of your colleagues is a Christian. . .and actively and regularly ask God to show you who it is.

Second, when you find that fellow believer, slowly build a rapport with him. In time, ask him to tell you his story. Most men will balk at first, but gently ask again and again if necessary. Then keep quiet and let him do all the talking.

Third, invite your Christian colleague to join you before work once a week for a brief time of Bible reading and prayer. Meet for half an hour before work starts, but keep the Bible reading and prayer time to eight or ten minutes. Watch how your lives flourish in new ways!

Lord, I'm asking You to show me which of my colleagues know You. Please give us a flourishing faith connection.

WEDNESDAY

PRAY FOR YOUR CHURCH'S STAFF

Pray also for me, that whenever I speak,
words may be given me so that I will fearlessly
make known the mystery of the gospel.
EPHESIANS 6:19 NIV

Who works at your church? The staff may include the pastor and a volunteer secretary. Or it may feature a senior pastor, executive pastor, associate pastor, music minister, youth minister, children's ministry director, and office manager. My church has five full- and part-time staff. My daughter's church has fifty. The important thing isn't the number of staff but who's praying regularly for them.

Church workers pray for their people, of course, but many struggle to pray for themselves. That's why they want and need *our* prayers. I like to pray for each one by name, and with a fairly good understanding of their job responsibilities. Then I make a point of writing thank-you cards for their ministry, mentioning my prayers on their behalf.

The same goes for those people my church has commissioned to serve overseas. They greatly appreciate encouraging notes, but mostly they're thankful that God hears and answers our prayers on their behalf.

Lord, help me to know my church's staff and their needs—and then to pray specifically for each one.

THURSDAY

PRAY FOR YOUR CHURCH'S M.I.A.

Therefore confess your sins to each other and pray for each other so that you may be healed. The prayer of a righteous person is powerful and effective.
JAMES 5:16 NIV

What do you think of senior citizens, middle-aged folks, and young adults who walk away from the church? Do things like "backslidden" or "probably not a Christian in the first place" come to mind? Have you ever considered other possibilities?

A twenty-six-year-old friend who lives a mile from us stopped going to church. Instead of judging, Renée and I called her. We found out she works some Sundays and needs a ride on others. What a delight to carpool together.

A seventy-something couple stopped coming to church. We had a great time getting together with them. We knew they traveled a lot. We didn't know they catch every Sunday service online. Great for them!

Years ago, another friend walked away from the church and his childhood Christian faith. Recently he and I had a great conversation about God's radical forgiveness. How good that the Lord wants all to come to repentance (2 Peter 3:9).

Lord, I thank You for Your faithful-when-we're-not love for each of us. Show me who's missing in action from my church, and help me to reach out in love.

FRIDAY

PRAY FOR GOD'S PEOPLE EVERYWHERE

Stay alert and be persistent in your prayers
for all believers everywhere.
EPHESIANS 6:18 NLT

After a terrible medical disaster, I spent two weeks in the hospital and four more weeks in rehab. One of the rehab nurses, Miriam, had emigrated to the United States from Ethiopia. She told me she was a member of the Ethiopian Orthodox Church. "I love Ethiopia," I replied. "I pray for your country every day and love the gifts Ethiopian Orthodoxy offers to the rest of the church." Miriam was overjoyed.

Through Compassion International, our family sponsors an eleven-year-old Ethiopian girl, Betselot, who lives in one of the ten cities adjacent to Ethiopia's capital. I pray regularly for her, her siblings, her parents, her school, her church, her city, and the peace and prosperity of her country.

I also pray regularly for the spiritual growth, endurance, maturity, and love of Christians in Muslim, Hindu, and Buddhist nations, and for God's protection over those who are at risk.

We may never serve the Lord overseas, but our prayers can reach around the world and make a difference.

Lord, please help me to pray for my Christian brothers and sisters everywhere. Today, show me a nation I can emphasize in my prayers.

Lord, I'm so thankful and glad that my prayers make a difference for my friends and acquaintances, and even people around the world.

5 TOPICS COVERED THIS WEEK:

MONDAY: pray for your Christian friends
TUESDAY: pray for your Christian colleagues
WEDNESDAY: pray for your church's staff
THURSDAY: pray for your church's M.I.A.
FRIDAY: pray for God's people everywhere

3 WAYS PRAYING FOR OTHERS ENERGIZES ME:

1.

2.

3.

3 WAYS PRAYING FOR OTHERS DRAINS ME:

1.

2.

3.

How I want to respond to these truths:

LORD, HERE'S WHAT'S GOING ON IN MY LIFE RIGHT NOW. . .

OTHER THINGS I NEED TO SHARE WITH YOU, LORD. . .

Lord, when it comes to this new life map, I need to. . .

Pray for all people. Ask God to help them; intercede on their behalf, and give thanks for them.

1 TIMOTHY 2:1 NLT

Thank You, Lord, for hearing my prayers and for helping me take action!

AMEN.

WEEK 5

BIBLE READING

Certain decisions can change the whole trajectory of your life. They can produce more positive results than you could possibly imagine from the outset. Here are three:

First, to become a wholehearted follower of Jesus Christ. Second, to become the right kind of man before finding and marrying your soulmate. Third, to read the Bible for at least five minutes every day.

I made all three of these commitments when I was thirteen. How radically different—how much poorer and sadder—my life would be without them. It hurts to envision such a gut-wrenching life, but believe me, I can imagine it quite easily. My family tree up to that point, along with my own behaviors, compelled me to make drastic changes to avoid a dismal future. I'm so glad I made all three decisions and then stuck with them.

Ready to make the third commitment? I hope so!

Instruct the wise and they will be wiser still; teach the righteous and they will add to their learning. The fear of the LORD is the beginning of wisdom, and knowledge of the Holy One is understanding. For through wisdom your days will be many, and years will be added to your life.

PROVERBS 9:9–11 NIV

MONDAY

BEFORE YOU READ THE BIBLE

"I have not departed from the commands of [God's] lips; I have treasured the words of his mouth more than my daily bread."
JOB 23:12 NIV

Before I go to bed at night, I know I have to do three things. Actually, I do more than that, but three are essentials: checking my blood sugar, taking my prescriptions, and storing my contact lenses for the night. Could I skip them? Yes, but only if I'm willing to miss out on the benefits.

Before I read the Bible each day, I also have three essentials. First is reverence for the Lord God, creator of heaven and earth, and the true author of scripture. The higher my regard for the Lord, the greater benefits I'll enjoy as I read His Word.

Second is respect for the Bible itself. This book was written with the Holy Spirit's inspiration by forty men over the course of sixteen hundred years. Thousands of other people copied, distributed, and preserved each book of the Bible. Other thousands translated it into the world's languages today.

Third is repentance of any known sin in my life before I start reading the Bible. I want the author of scripture to speak to me freely.

Lord, I thank You for providing Your Word in English. Please speak to me as I read it!

TUESDAY

READING THE BIBLE FOR THE FIRST TIME

They read from the Book of the Law of God,
making it clear and giving the meaning so that
the people understood what was being read.
NEHEMIAH 8:8 NIV

The first time I read the Joseph story in Genesis, I couldn't believe how harshly it started out. I was relieved when Joseph was released from slavery and prison. I cheered when he rose in power in Egypt, second only to Pharaoh.

It didn't surprise me that Joseph hid his identity when his brothers came to Egypt—the brothers who had originally sold him into slavery. They wanted to buy grain for their families experiencing famine back in Canaan. I have to admit that I smiled when Joseph spoke harshly to the men.

By the time I started reading Genesis 45, I sensed Joseph's revenge was right around the corner. In the climactic moment, when Joseph revealed his true identity, I expected the brothers to be slaughtered like pigs—but instead, Joseph forgave them, and I broke down and wept. After all they had done to him years earlier, how could he? I didn't see that coming.

When you read the Bible, read to learn—and read to be moved emotionally. If your emotions are engaged, you'll remember what you read for months and years and decades to come.

Lord, please move me as I read Your Word.

WEDNESDAY

HOW DO I START READING THE BIBLE?

So then faith comes by hearing,
and hearing by the word of God.
ROMANS 10:17 NKJV

Made a pledge to read the Bible daily? Here are steps to help you:

1. Set a goal, for example, to read from Genesis 1 to Revelation 22 in a year. Then select a personal reward for accomplishing that goal. If you finish early, all the better.
2. Divide and conquer. You can finish the entire Bible in twelve months by reading about fifteen minutes at a shot, roughly three chapters a day. Can't make it every day? Then read twenty minutes (about four chapters) five days a week. Find yourself caught up in a passage? It's okay to read ahead a bit so you can take a break later on.
3. Read with your head *and* heart. If you don't understand something, it's okay to ask questions. But as you read, focus on what is clear. Look for (a) examples to heed, (b) truths to believe, and (c) commands to obey.
4. Pick a favorite verse to make your own. My wife and I chose Psalm 34:3 for our marriage. A good friend picked 1 Thessalonians 3:13 as a prayer focus for the year.

Lord, I thank You that reading the Bible becomes easier with time. Thanks for the privilege I have to read it daily.

THURSDAY

CHOOSE A BIBLE READING PLAN

Jesus answered, "It is written: 'Man shall not live on bread alone, but on every word that comes from the mouth of God.'"

MATTHEW 4:4 NIV

The one way *not* to read the Bible is to open it randomly and jump into a passage. I suppose it's better than nothing—but surely we can do better than that. Here are much better options:

1. Read highlights from every book. You can digest important excerpts from Genesis to Revelation in two months.
2. Read highlights about every important person from Adam to Zechariah. In four months' time, you can become acquainted with the entire Who's Who of scripture.
3. Read the whole Bible from Genesis to Revelation. As we saw earlier, it takes only fifteen minutes a day.
4. Read the whole Bible in the order each event or writing took place. With this approach, you'll see the historical links between various parts of the Bible.

You can find each of these reading plans at biblegateway.com/reading-plans/more. Enjoy!

Lord, I thank You for the variety of ways I can read Your Word. Which option should I choose?

FRIDAY

READ WITH GOD AT WORK INSIDE YOU

I have hidden your word in my heart that
I might not sin against you.
PSALM 119:11 NIV

When we read the Bible, we need to do so with our spiritual eyes wide open. How do we do that?

First, go to God in prayer. We can worship God, thank Him for His Word, and ask Him to remove anything that would cloud our hearts and minds as we read the Bible.

Next, ask God for the Holy Spirit's illumination as you read (and reread) each passage of scripture. We can read the same section of the Bible twenty, thirty, or forty times (or more) and still make new discoveries with each reading.

Finally, approach the Bible with a strong sense of expectancy, determination, and persistence. We need to look closely at scripture. The goal of such careful observation is to discover more and more of what God's Word says.

We're not conducting a superficial once-over, a cursory glance for some trivial tidbit. We're talking about looking intently at scripture and asking God to change us accordingly.

Lord, I thank You for all the good You do inside me when I read Your Word. I'm thrilled!

Lord, You not only spoke the word to create the heavens and earth, but You also spoke the Word to some forty men who wrote down the inspired scripture. Thank You!

5 TOPICS COVERED THIS WEEK:

MONDAY: before you read the Bible
TUESDAY: reading the Bible for the first time
WEDNESDAY: how do I start reading the Bible?
THURSDAY: choose a Bible reading plan
FRIDAY: read with God at work inside you

3 WAYS BIBLE READING LIFTS ME:

1 ....

2 ....

3 ....

3 WAYS BIBLE READING DEFLATES ME:

1 ....

2 ....

3 ....

How I want to respond to these truths:

....

....

....

....

....

....

....

....

LORD, HERE'S WHAT'S GOING ON IN MY LIFE RIGHT NOW. . .

OTHER THINGS I NEED TO SHARE WITH YOU, LORD. . .

Lord, when it comes to this new life map, I need to. . .

Open my eyes that I may see wonderful things in your law.

PSALM 119:18 NIV

Thank You, Lord, for hearing my prayers and for helping me take action!

AMEN.

WEEK 6

BIBLE STUDY

Have you ever become painfully aware of a certain truth, but then chose to ignore (or conveniently forget) it?

We humans have an amazing capacity for knowing truth but going on our merry way as if we can somehow defy the odds, as if nature is obligated to make exceptions for us, as if reality will change to accommodate our forgetfulness or willfulness or stubbornness or arrogance.

It's amazing how, in this day of phenomenal technological advance and the explosion of knowledge, we humans can so easily ignore the obvious, the known, the true. It's as if common sense has been laid aside in favor of the latest fashions or fads.

Reality, however, has a way of slapping us in the face. No matter our age, education, social status, income, and net worth, reality allows no exceptions. And here is reality: God exists, He created our world, and He has certain expectations of us.

Of first importance, then, is our study of what the Lord says in His Word, the Bible.

> *"Keep this Book of the Law always on your lips; meditate on it day and night, so that you may be careful to do everything written in it. Then you will be prosperous and successful."*
> Joshua 1:8 niv

MONDAY

TRUTHS TO AFFIRM

For the word of God is alive and active.
Sharper than any double-edged sword, it penetrates
even to dividing soul and spirit, joints and marrow;
it judges the thoughts and attitudes of the heart.
Hebrews 4:12 niv

When you begin to read the Bible, it doesn't take long to discover it's full of literary genres. Within the thirty-nine books of the Hebrew scriptures (the Old Testament) and the twenty-seven Christian scriptures (the New Testament), you'll find historical accounts, poetry, laws, prophecy, and more. How do you make sense of it all?

Here's an approach: TA-CO, EH! It works from Mexico to Canada (everywhere, really). TA stands for "truths to affirm." CO stands for "commands to obey." And EH stands for "examples to heed."

As you read a section of scripture, simply ask yourself three questions. First, are there any truths to affirm? Second, are there any commands to obey? And third, are there any examples to heed?

The Bible is full of truths, but some have greater impact on our lives. The most important ones teach realities about the Lord God. The more we know and affirm them, the greater He will bless our lives.

Can you make it a goal to affirm at least ten valuable biblical truths today?

Lord, I thank You for filling the Bible with important truths. I believe them!

TUESDAY

COMMANDS TO OBEY

All Scripture is breathed out by God and profitable for teaching, for reproof, for correction, and for training in righteousness, that the man of God may be complete, equipped for every good work.

2 Timothy 3:16–17 esv

Yesterday, I introduced the TA-CO, EH! acronym. CO stands for "commands to obey." Would it surprise you to learn that the Bible isn't full of commands? A thousand-page Bible has two commands per page—and nearly half don't apply to you and me today.

For instance, the apostle Paul commanded his protégé, Timothy, "No longer drink only water, but use a little wine for the sake of your stomach and your frequent ailments" (1 Timothy 5:23 esv). That was never intended for every Christian.

On the other hand, we guys are too apt to assign "not applicable" status to commands that *do* apply to all Christians of all time.

Take what Paul says a minute later to Timothy: "Some people, eager for money, have wandered from the faith and pierced themselves with many griefs. But you, man of God, flee from all this" (1 Timothy 6:10–11 niv). This injunction echoes what is taught by Moses and many others throughout scripture, including Jesus, multiple times.

Applicable to you and me? Yes!

Lord, I thank You for Your commands, which provide both a fence of protection and much freedom.

WEDNESDAY

EXAMPLES TO HEED

For everything that was written in the past was written to teach us, so that through the endurance taught in the Scriptures and the encouragement they provide we might have hope.

ROMANS 15:4 NIV

We're now at the end of the TA-CO, EH! acronym. EH stands for "examples to heed." Some have asked why I don't say "examples to *follow*." That's because so many of the examples in the Old and New Testaments are negative.

Consider young David's amazing confession of faith in the Lord God, creator of heaven and earth, right before he fought Goliath (1 Samuel 17:45–47). Oh, to make such a confession today! But then take the older David's decision to betray and murder one of his thirty "mighty men," Uriah, and steal the man's wife (2 Samuel 11). In doing so, David broke nearly half of the Ten Commandments. May you and I never do the same.

How wonderful to remember Jesus was never hypocritical. He didn't just *say*, "Walk a second mile"; He did it. Jesus didn't just *say*, "Turn the other cheek"; He did when He was slapped. . .hard. Jesus taught people to give up their shirt and coat. . .then gave up His own life for us. His is an example worth following!

Lord, thank You for the positive and negative examples in scripture. May I gladly imitate and follow Jesus today.

THURSDAY

APPLICATION VIA MEDITATION

His delight is in the law of the Lord,
and on his law he meditates day and night.
Psalm 1:2 ESV

Without application, the Bible makes no more difference in your life than water in a cooler, coffee behind the counter, or a fruit-flavored energy drink in a television commercial. There's no benefit unless you take it in.

That's why it's so important to *meditate* on scripture. It's not enough just to read words on the page. You and I need to wash our minds with God's Word. Meditation can involve:

- reflecting on the meaning of key words in a paragraph, verse, sentence, or phrase;
- memorizing a section of God's Word; or even
- rewriting a scripture passage in your own words.

James 1:25 (ESV) reminds us that "the one who looks into the perfect law, the law of liberty, and perseveres, being no hearer who forgets but a doer who acts, he will be blessed in his doing."

Throughout scripture, God has promised to bless the person who reads His Word, considers it intently, interprets it correctly. . .then personalizes and applies it to his life.

Lord, please help me to read, reflect on,
and memorize scripture—then do what it says.

FRIDAY

WRESTLING WITH UNANSWERED QUESTIONS

Your word is a lamp for my feet, a light on my path.
PSALM 119:105 NIV

As we read the Bible, we need to keep asking, "What did God mean by this statement?" As you go through scripture, write down your questions. Reading the Bible isn't a matter of *our* interpretation. Instead, you and I want to embrace the orthodox understanding of God's Word—that is, the established views of the larger Christian church throughout history.

If you don't have a study Bible, it's time to buy one. You might want to check out some Bible commentaries too. But know that not all commentaries are created equal. If you're reading one (or any resource) that doesn't (1) worship God, (2) praise the Lord Jesus Christ, and (3) show tremendous respect for God's Word, drop it fast and look for a better one!

Do your best to discover what God wants you to know. Most of the answers to our questions are right there in His Word. In the end, however, it's okay to have some unanswered questions. In those cases, we'll have to wait until heaven to ask Moses, David, Ezra, or Paul, "What did you mean by that?"

**Lord, thanks for welcoming tough questions.
Help me to dig deeply into Your Word for answers.**

DATE:

Lord, this week I learned not only what to look for when I read the Bible (TA-CO, EH!), but also how to go the second mile so Your Word makes a difference in my heart and mind.

5 TOPICS COVERED THIS WEEK:

MONDAY: truths to affirm
TUESDAY: commands to obey
WEDNESDAY: examples to heed
THURSDAY: application via meditation
FRIDAY: wrestling with unanswered questions

3 WAYS BIBLE TRUTHS ANCHOR ME:

1 ....

2 ....

3 ....

3 WAYS BIBLE PASSAGES CONFUSE ME:

1 ....

2 ....

3 ....

How I want to respond to these truths:

LORD, HERE'S WHAT'S GOING ON IN MY LIFE RIGHT NOW. . .

OTHER THINGS I NEED TO SHARE WITH YOU, LORD. . .

Lord, when it comes to this new life map, I need to. . .

Do not merely listen to the word, and so deceive yourselves. Do what it says.

JAMES 1:22 NIV

Thank You, Lord, for hearing my prayers and for helping me take action!

AMEN.

WEEK 7

CHURCH ATTENDANCE

Every man who follows Jesus Christ is a member of God's kingdom, God's family, and God's church. The last two chapters of Revelation celebrate the future realities of all three. Here and now, though, Jesus calls us to be active members of a local expression of His church.

We sometimes forget that the church is the Lord's idea. Jesus founded it so His followers could more effectively make disciples by teaching His commandments, offering water baptism, and reminding them that He is "with you always, to the very end of the age" (Matthew 28:20 NIV).

I live in Portland, Oregon, often described as one of the least-churched cities in America. . .though there are some fourteen hundred even here! I spent years gathering stories about why people had left the church. All were valid for leaving a given church, but not for leaving *the church*.

This week, discover how you can bless—and be blessed by—God's church.

If I am delayed, you will know how people ought to conduct themselves in God's household, which is the church of the living God, the pillar and foundation of the truth.

1 Timothy 3:15 NIV

MONDAY

VISIT ALL KINDS OF CHURCHES

In Christ we, though many, form one body,
and each member belongs to all the others.
ROMANS 12:5 NIV

In our family, moving to a new city has been a great opportunity to visit churches from A to Z. Attending different churches for a while may sound daunting, but only for the first few weeks. When else do you have such a great opportunity to see the bigger church in action?

The reality is that every denomination has gifts for the rest of the church. What a joy to be blessed—directly or indirectly—by some of those gifts. Conversely, every denomination has a few customs or traditions that may feel peculiar to you. That's okay. In most cases, it's not wrong, just different.

Some denominations carry a rich sense of history. Some follow the church calendar and offer liturgy. Some provide a deep theological tradition. Some support robust ministries locally, regionally, nationally, or overseas. Some proclaim the gospel in some form every Sunday.

The more you love Jesus Christ's bride, the church, the more you love Jesus Himself.

Lord, I thank You for all the opportunities I have to see the bigger church in action.

TUESDAY

NARROW YOUR OPTIONS

Preach the word; be prepared in season and out of season; correct, rebuke and encourage—with great patience and careful instruction.
2 Timothy 4:2 NIV

After visiting a wide range of churches, it's important to decide which ones most appeal to you. In our family, criteria include preaching, music, ministries, theological compatibility, and openhandedness. The latter is a church's willingness to allow for differences on second- and third-level doctrinal matters. We have plenty of differences within our family, after all, and want a church that allows for them. But when it comes to the core of orthodoxy, our family is 100 percent in agreement.

Think of the larger church—the overall "body of Christ"—like a tree. It has a lot of branches that stretch around the world and roots that go down through the centuries. Some members of our family belong to Anabaptist churches and others to Reformed congregations. (Interestingly, centuries ago, one of those branches persecuted the other quite harshly.)

Today, choosing a local church is both an objective issue (is it biblical?) and a subjective matter (is it a good fit?). In other words, you have a lot of freedom—so enjoy the process.

Lord, I thank You for the freedom to attend and join a church that both honors You and welcomes me.

WEDNESDAY

PLANT YOUR ROOTS DEEPLY

Have confidence in your leaders and submit to their authority, because they keep watch over you as those who must give an account. Do this so that their work will be a joy, not a burden, for that would be of no benefit to you.

HEBREWS 13:17 NIV

I don't want to give the impression that our family flits like butterflies from church to church. After a trial period, we make a final decision and plant our roots deeply into a local church body.

In making our decision, we first look over the church's history and statement of faith. Then we get to know its staff and leadership structure. Third, we make a commitment to attend services every weekend. Fourth, we join a small group for fellowship, prayer, and Bible study. Fifth, we practice hospitality. Finally, after six months, we join—offering to serve in one or more ministries.

Of course, there can be too much of a good thing. When one of our older children couldn't decide between two churches, he mapped out their schedules and planned to attend different services every week at both. That may sound super spiritual, but it's impossible to plant roots deeply in different places at the same time. Flip a coin if necessary—but choose one church!

Lord, I'm grateful that You created the church as a place where I can grow and thrive. Show me how to contribute to its success.

THURSDAY

TWO VERY IMPORTANT INSIGHTS

Then the church. . .enjoyed a time of peace and was strengthened. Living in the fear of the Lord and encouraged by the Holy Spirit, it increased in numbers.
ACTS 9:31 NIV

For twenty years my spiritual father and mentor, the evangelist Luis Palau, kept busy answering my questions and giving me lots of books to read. At one point, of course, we started talking about how he and his family had planted their roots deeply into one of Portland's many hundreds of churches.

I'll never forget two things Luis said. First, "By neglecting to minister within your local church, you cause other Christians to lose something. The Lord Jesus Himself says in John 15:5 that He is the vine, and we are connected to Him as branches. As a result, through Jesus, we are connected to each other. We are members of His body, the church." Second, Luis added: "In 1 Corinthians 12:26 [NIV] we read, 'If one part suffers, every part suffers with it; if one part is honored, every part rejoices with it.' How you relate or fail to relate to the body of Christ directly affects other Christians. We need each other!"

Lord, You created the church to be a place where You're tangibly at work. I'm thankful that I can belong to Your family in a real way.

FRIDAY

THREE MORE INSIGHTS

Let us consider how we may spur one another on toward love and good deeds, not giving up meeting together, as some are in the habit of doing, but encouraging one another—and all the more as you see the Day approaching.
HEBREWS 10:24–25 NIV

I'll never forget three more things Luis Palau told me.

First, "When my family is ready to leave for church, we take certain expectations about what we want to get and leave them home with the dog. Consequently, everything we do receive is a blessing. We're not there to get, but to give."

Second, Luis added: "It is important to speak well of *our* church. Let your children hear you talking about *our* pastor, *our* elders, *our* deacons, *our* Sunday school, *our* church retreat. This will help them claim the church as their own as they grow older."

Third, Luis made a point of saying that his particular church wasn't the biggest or best, and probably never would be. That didn't matter. What did matter was that it was his family's home church for the long haul.

Lord, thank You for creating the church to be a place where I can grow and thrive. Help me to bless and be blessed.

Lord, You call me to be an active member of a local expression of Your church. I want to discover how I can bless—and be blessed—through that local body.

5 TOPICS COVERED THIS WEEK:

MONDAY: visit all kinds of churches
TUESDAY: narrow your options
WEDNESDAY: plant your roots deeply
THURSDAY: two very important insights
FRIDAY: three more insights

3 WAYS CHURCH BENEFITS ME:

1 ……………………………………

2 ……………………………………

3 ……………………………………

3 WAYS CHURCH HAS HURT ME:

1 ……………………………………

2 ……………………………………

3 ……………………………………

How I want to respond to these truths:

……………………………………

……………………………………

……………………………………

……………………………………

……………………………………

……………………………………

……………………………………

……………………………………

LORD, HERE'S WHAT'S GOING ON IN MY LIFE RIGHT NOW. . .

OTHER THINGS I NEED TO SHARE WITH YOU, LORD. . .

Lord, when it comes to this new life map, I need to. . .

You are a chosen people, a royal priesthood, a holy nation, God's special possession, that you may declare the praises of him who called you out of darkness into his wonderful light.

1 PETER 2:9 NIV

Thank You, Lord, for hearing my prayers and for helping me take action!

AMEN.

WEEK 8

FAMILY, PART 1

Though some people remain single throughout life, most will marry. Family starts when God calls a man and woman to wed and then live together as "one flesh" (Genesis 2:24). Teamwork would seem to be a natural by-product. But what does it mean to be a team?

For couples who share similar tastes, gifts, goals, and desires, teamwork is as smooth as pairs figure skating. They go through life hand in hand, moving together to the same music.

Other couples find their partnership is more like a track and field team. They're on the same team, but their lives are individual events. Though they're gifted and impassioned differently, they support and cheer each other on in their individual struggles and successes.

Sometimes a couple's marriage resembles a car race. The drivers are the stars of the show, but they wouldn't win anything without the pit crew's efforts at every stop.

Think about your interests and personalities. What kind of team would best represent you and your (possibly future) wife's relationship? You'll learn a lot this week!

Over all these [Christian] virtues put on love,
which binds them all together in perfect unity.
COLOSSIANS 3:14 NIV

MONDAY

AGREE ON SACRIFICES

Let no debt remain outstanding, except the continuing debt to love one another, for whoever loves others has fulfilled the law.

ROMANS 13:8 NIV

Similarities alone don't produce a good marriage partnership. What does? A strong commitment to each other's personal growth and a deep commitment to oneness before God. This week we'll look at five strategies my wife and I—and some of our closest friends—have used along the way.

The first strategy is most important: agree in advance on any sacrifices. Our friends Paul and Wendy have a beautiful backyard, but the years have not been a bed of roses! When he wanted to go back to school, it was a decision they made together. To prevent resentment, they consciously outlined what sacrifices they would (and wouldn't) make to realize Paul's goal of earning a doctorate in psychology.

They decided they *could* live with Wendy's almost full-time job out of their home and the need to live frugally. They *would not* accept drifting apart as a couple or shortchanging their time with their children. Paul and Wendy reached the other side with a strong marriage and family—and Wendy has learned a lot of counseling skills too!

Lord, what sacrifices would please You the most? Please make them clear to both of us.

TUESDAY

DREAM TOGETHER

Love never gives up, never loses faith,
[and] is always hopeful.
1 CORINTHIANS 13:7 NLT

One marriage expert recommends that, on their anniversary each year, couples take one hour to dream together. He believes this will increase the longevity and happiness of a marriage. We agree.

Dreaming together deepens the spirit of partnership. Wherever the winds may blow us, we remember we are on the same ship. This kind of dreaming brought Renée and me to the place of adopting our youngest daughter, Anna. Now we're enjoying grandkids! Dreaming together has also taken us to the Alps, the Andes, the Amazon, and Africa to visit beloved missionary friends. Next stop: Australia or Antarctica?

Be willing to encourage and follow each other's dreams too. Who knows where your spouse's next dream could take you? When I began dreaming about the two of us writing notes for the *Living Faith Bible*, Renée happily went along. She actually agreed to write three-fourths of the notes—and says she had the time of her life doing it.

Lord, which of my dreams do You want me to share with my wife? And which dreams do You want me to lay aside, at least for now?

WEDNESDAY

CREATE A MISSION STATEMENT

Let me hear of your unfailing love each morning, for I am trusting you. Show me where to walk, for I give myself to you.
PSALM 143:8 NLT

A mission statement transforms dreams and desires into a tool you can grasp and use. Later, as needed, you can make revisions.

To create your mission statement, invite your wife to take some time away with you. This could be a weekend getaway, or it could occur over the course of several dates. Categorize your individual gifts and passions in life. Make a list of your mutual desires and goals. Prioritize your time and talents—both as individuals and as a couple. Consider how you can use your differences to accomplish the mutual goals. Above all, pray for God to show you *His* desires. Ask Him to give you a mission by which to guide your marriage, both now and in the future.

Creating a mission statement helped our friends Troy and Shannon to thoughtfully say no to the constant moves that his career demanded. When he was diagnosed with cancer, their written purpose and priorities kept their marriage vision crystal clear. When the disease claimed Troy's life, that mission statement was an incredible testimony to those who attended his memorial service.

Lord, please help us to create a mission statement that honors You.

THURSDAY

DIVIDE AND CONQUER

Let love and faithfulness never leave you; bind them around your neck, write them on the tablet of your heart.

PROVERBS 3:3 NIV

Having similar gifts and callings is no guarantee that teamwork will flow naturally. When Renée and I were first married, I would take on classes for the two of us to teach "together." That translated into me giving her an outline or a script of what she should say. She balked because it felt artificial. It *was* artificial!

By the time we began working on the *Living Faith Bible*, however, we had learned to truly work together. We had a mutual goal but maintained our own autonomy. And still today, we divide the work and then each of us has full authority over our own portion of the project. When Renée writes something, I can suggest specific things she might consider adding, deleting, or changing—but she always gets the final say. For us, that feels like teamwork.

Many couples "divide and conquer" when it comes to the daily to-do list of home and family life. Ideally, you and your wife can focus on areas of personal strength and interest. When Renée went back to the university, I took over the laundry, but she kept cooking. That way, we were both happy.

Lord, show us how to divide and conquer as a couple—from our daily tasks to our largest goals and dreams.

FRIDAY

NURTURE YOUR TEAM SPIRIT

Above all, love each other deeply,
because love covers over a multitude of sins.
1 PETER 4:8 NIV

What should you do when "divide" leaves you feeling stuck with too much of the work? And what about when "conquer" doesn't happen because you or your wife are overwhelmed by other stresses in life? That's when the spirit of "team" transcends the "work" in *teamwork*.

Sometimes all I need is God's reminder that we are, indeed, teammates—not opponents. Ultimately, Renée and I both want the same thing: to love God, to love each other, to love our children, to grow as people, and to live in peace. Other times, when I have felt my team spirit waning, I pray more earnestly for Renée. Talking to God and asking Him to bless and help my wife realigns my heart with hers—and with God's.

Occasional selfish squabbles aside, Renée and I build our marriage partnership best when we heed God's calling. It's a calling to look not only to our own interests, but to the interests of others; to consider another as better than ourselves; and to lay down our lives for our very best, lifelong friend—our mate.

Lord, how can I best nurture and support my wife?
Guide me in Your way, and help me to act.

Lord, I thank You that family starts when You call a man and woman to wed and then live together as "one flesh." Thanks too for what I'm learning about marriage.

5 TOPICS COVERED THIS WEEK:

MONDAY: agree on sacrifices
TUESDAY: dream together
WEDNESDAY: create a mission statement
THURSDAY: divide and conquer
FRIDAY: nurture your team spirit

3 WAYS MARRIAGE EMPOWERS ME:

1 ....

2 ....

3 ....

3 WAYS MARRIAGE BAFFLES ME:

1 ....

2 ....

3 ....

How I want to respond to these truths:

....

....

....

....

....

....

....

....

LORD, HERE'S WHAT'S GOING ON IN MY LIFE RIGHT NOW. . .

OTHER THINGS I NEED TO SHARE WITH YOU, LORD. . .

Lord, when it comes to this new life map, I need to. . .

So God created mankind in his own image, in the image of God he created them; male and female he created them.

GENESIS 1:27 NIV

Thank You, Lord, for hearing my prayers and for helping me take action!

AMEN.

WEEK 9

FAMILY, PART 2

God created Adam and Eve and called them to bring children into the world. Since then, each person finds his or her place in this experience called "family." Where do you find yourself in this continuum: grandson, son, brother, husband, uncle?

You can't escape the impact of the family you came from, but you can create strength in a family, whatever your role. That's true whether or not you have children, whether you live alone or with several generations. God can grow you through your family relationships.

Say "family," and for most people strong emotions arise. What kind of wisdom and planning can bring more joy and peace and growth to your family relationships? Let's explore that this week!

"Choose today whom you will serve. . . .
As for me and my family, we will serve the LORD."
JOSHUA 24:15 NLT

MONDAY

HONOR YOUR PARENTS

"Honor your father and mother"—which is the first commandment with a promise—"so that it may go well with you and that you may enjoy long life on the earth."
EPHESIANS 6:2–3 NIV

My wife's parents saved her life. They trusted God and made choices to provide her with the safe, loving home that they themselves had not experienced as children. My adopted daughter's parents destroyed her home—her good life now is the result of many years of love, commitment, and hard work.

You can't escape where you came from, but you can make new paths for yourself and your family. Begin by recognizing your identity within God's family. Do the work of acceptance and forgiveness.

If your parents are still living, your responsibility is to treat them as human beings made in the image of God—and loved by Him. Honoring them means acknowledging the gift of life they gave you. Ask God what He wants in your relationship with your parents, and then consider the following: What message can you tell yourself that honors your parents? What words can you say to your parents that will show them honor?

Father, help me to show honor to the parents who gave me life. May I extend the same kind of love You have shown to me.

TUESDAY

BABY MAKES THREE

Children are a gift from the Lord;
they are a reward from him.
Psalm 127:3 NLT

Nothing changes things like a little person entering your world to stay. Your heart is full, your body is tired, and life is completely upended!

From the moment you first lock eyes, delight in him. Each time you respond to his cries and meet his needs, you build his ability to trust. Put down the phone, turn off the game, and give your full attention. Remember: he's a child—and only for a short while. He's immature because he's young. He's needy because he's small.

Books, podcasts, and classes can all give information on how to raise a child, but ultimately *you* will be the expert on this unique human being. You'll make mistakes, but you'll learn as you go. Take time, today and every day, to know your children personally. They need nurture and discipline specific to themselves.

And always, *always*, trust the Lord. Never forget that children are a gift, not a possession. God loves your kid(s) more than you possibly could, yet He chose *you* to be this child's father. And God makes no mistakes.

Lord, children are an incredible blessing—and challenge. Help me to love mine the way You love me!

WEDNESDAY

THE LONGEST, FASTEST EIGHTEEN YEARS

These commandments that I give you today are to be on your hearts. Impress them on your children.

DEUTERONOMY 6:6–7 NIV

When you're a parent, it seems like childhood will never end—until it does. Days are filled with getting the kids fed, clothed, and educated, driving them to play dates, music lessons, and sporting events. How do you find the time and energy to raise responsible, healthy, loving human beings?

Choose your family values and communicate them often—and live them out yourself. Live so that one day your children may say, "My father always. . ."! They can't escape your words and habits.

Create good boundaries. Children need the safety of family rules and appropriate discipline. Your children need *you* to be the parent—they're not ready to be in charge.

But open doorways as they grow. Celebrate achievements. Give more responsibility, and allow them to make more of their own choices each year. Children need to feel confident on their own.

Build a village within your church family, neighborhood, or school district. Your child needs others to model, encourage, and fill in the gaps. Parenting isn't a solo journey.

Through it all, pray for your kids. God molds their hearts.

Lord, strengthen me to guide my children so that they may be the people we both want them to be.

THURSDAY

LOVING SOMEONE ELSE'S CHILD

"Whoever welcomes one of these little children in my name welcomes me."

MARK 9:37 NIV

When my wife was a girl, her parents fostered a child, welcomed refugees from Vietnam, and adopted both her oldest brother and two younger sisters. My mother provided daycare and nurture for neighborhood children and drove countless more to church each week. Some homes are hubs for kids who need a place where they are listened to and loved.

God's heart beats strong for children. Jesus welcomed them with delight, and made it clear to His disciples that He expected them to do the same. Whether or not you're a "kid person," God wants you to welcome children too. Not just your own, but other people's.

What might happen if you said yes to God today? Start in the church nursery or teaching Sunday school, become a volunteer in your local school, or take a niece or nephew to lunch so your sister can have a break.

Or jump in deep—foster or adopt a waiting child. It takes making room in your home, your lifestyle, and your heart. But you'll be welcoming Jesus too.

Lord, I want to welcome You. Show me how to welcome a child who needs me.

FRIDAY

FRIENDS ARE FAMILY YOU CHOOSE

There is a friend who sticks closer than a brother.
PROVERBS 18:24 NIV

For most of history, a man had few options outside family, farm work, and conscripted military service. Today, men enjoy many opportunities to create lives for themselves—and face the many responsibilities that accompany such opportunities.

In a world that's so big and yet so small, so connected and yet so isolating, a man needs God, who never changes and who will never leave him. And a man needs friends to love and be loved by.

I am blessed with a wonderful family and have nurtured select friends who have become family too. As I've grown and matured, I've learned what kind of people I need to be with and how I can give to others. I can accept people without needing them to be perfect or meet all my needs. I can enjoy what each friend has to offer and give my best to him.

Make the commitment to share life together with friends. Enjoy upbeat occasions in each other's homes. Be real (and available) in the hard times. Pray for each other. Be fiercely loyal. Be family.

Lord, I need You, and I need other people.
Show me whom I can make a true friend.

*Lord, I'm so glad You invented the family—
parents, children, even the friends we make in
this life. I will welcome and honor each one.*

5 TOPICS COVERED THIS WEEK:

MONDAY: honor your parents
TUESDAY: baby makes three
WEDNESDAY: the longest, fastest eighteen years
THURSDAY: loving someone else's child
FRIDAY: friends are family you choose

3 WAYS FAMILY BLESSES ME:

1 ....

2 ....

3 ....

3 WAYS FAMILY DRAINS ME:

1 ....

2 ....

3 ....

How I want to respond to these truths:

....

....

....

....

....

....

....

....

LORD, HERE'S WHAT'S GOING ON IN MY LIFE RIGHT NOW. . .

OTHER THINGS I NEED TO SHARE WITH YOU, LORD. . .

Lord, when it comes to this new life map, I need to. . .

Father of the fatherless and protector of widows is God in his holy habitation.

PSALM 68:5 ESV

Thank You, Lord, for hearing my prayers and for helping me take action!

AMEN.

WEEK 10

HOSPITALITY

How important is hospitality in your home?

Let's start with the people related to you. Many families have a hard time eating a single meal together each week, let alone every day. This despite extensive research showing the make-or-break factor in the average preteen's life is having at least five meals together with family each week.

Down through the ages, in most cultures around the world, eating meals together has been the fabric of life. It's how life is lived within families, neighborhoods, and other spheres of relationship. We certainly see this in the lives of the biblical heroes of the faith, as well as the ancient Jewish people. The latter celebrated Sabbath meals, other religious get-togethers, and at least three multi-day national festivals each year.

Jesus and His apostles ate together often, as did the early believers who followed them. They also invited a wide assortment of other people to join in.

Hospitality is an expected part of each Christian's character and way of life. This week, let's make it a bigger part of your life too.

While Jesus was having dinner at Matthew's house, many tax collectors and sinners came and ate with him and his disciples.

MATTHEW 9:10 NIV

MONDAY

HOST YOUR PASTOR FOR DINNER

The jailer brought them into his house and set a meal before them; he was filled with joy because he had come to believe in God—he and his whole household.
ACTS 16:34 NIV

As a church leader, I love inviting myself over to visit members of my congregation. In one case, the man and I had been conversing amiably for a while before he looked down and complained, "I don't like it that I've been attending the church for years and no pastor has ever visited me."

After a few seconds, it became clear he wasn't pulling my leg. I smiled and said, "Are you saying I'm not a pastor?"

"No. . .I mean, yes," he mumbled. Apparently, I didn't count! I had to laugh. Then again, pastors do the same thing themselves. Unless someone says "Pastor David" five times, I don't feel like a member has invited me specifically *because* I'm a pastor.

Today, why not invite your pastor over for dinner? And be sure to say "Pastor" five times. You might add, "I'm specifically inviting you over to thank you for serving as one of our church's pastors."

Lord, I thank You for the pastors in my life.
Give me the courage to reach out to one of them today.

TUESDAY

HOST A MISSIONARY FOR DINNER

When she and the members of her household were baptized, she invited us to her home. "If you consider me a believer in the Lord," she said, "come and stay at my house." And she persuaded us.

ACTS 16:15 NIV

I was led to the Lord by a missionary. Our family has enjoyed befriending missionaries who have served the Lord all over the world—even in Antarctica. Renée and I wanted to raise missions-minded children, so we loved inviting missionaries over for dinner whenever they were home on furlough.

Our missionary friends usually knew to focus on our kids, not the two of us. That sometimes meant bringing their country's flag, popular children's candies, and other objects for our children to see, smell, touch, and taste. In later years, it also meant having ten or fifteen colorful photos handy on their mobile phone.

Our missionary friends also knew to spend time letting our children take them around the house, including spinning our globe to show where they lived and served the Lord. And no evening was complete without our making time to pray together for the missionaries and their ministry. Be watching for such opportunities for your own family.

Lord, I thank You for the missionaries my church supports. Remind me this week to find out who's coming home on furlough.

WEDNESDAY

INVITE THE POOR

"But when you give a banquet, invite the poor."
LUKE 14:13 NIV

Some people love meeting new people. . .but most of us prefer to stick to the friends we know, especially when it comes to sharing our time and homes. Jesus, though, bluntly told us to invite the uninvited. In the verse above, that means people whose income level keeps them out of regular social circles.

You probably know people who struggle financially. Make sure to include them on the guest lists of your summer barbeques or holiday parties. Make every effort to diminish nervousness—theirs or yours. Get to know them as individuals. Find out where they come from and what they enjoy. Be unshockable if they reveal what they lack—and be ready with cash (not a check) to quietly meet at least one specific need. The Lord promises to reward you.

Ask your church leaders for ideas, and they will be glad to help you know whom to bless.

Lord, I praise You for Your love of each person, no matter their economic status. Please give me that same love.

THURSDAY

HOST A DISABLED PERSON

"But when you give a banquet, invite. . .
the crippled, the lame, the blind."
LUKE 14:13 NIV

After a routine back surgery went terribly wrong, I hung on for life for two weeks in wracking pain and near immobility. Then I was transferred to a rehab center where I spent four weeks slowly relearning how to sit and stand. Then I was taught the use of a wheelchair and walker.

By the time I returned to church, I was using a cane. Every time people said they wanted to hug me but were afraid of hurting me, I had to laugh. Nothing about my condition should interfere with our interactions, I said, except this: I couldn't accept invitations to homes with lots of stairs.

Think about the physical layout of your home, both inside and out. Ask your disabled friends if it's manageable. If so, smile and invite them to join you for dinner. When they arrive, simply offer an arm or a hand. If they take it, great! If not, let them manage on their own.

Dinner at your home will probably be the highlight of their week—and yours too.

Lord, I thank You for gladly eating with (and healing!)
the sick, crippled, lame, and blind. Show me a
disabled person You'd like me to invite over.

FRIDAY

HOST AN IMMIGRANT FOR DINNER

He defends the cause of the fatherless and the widow, and loves the foreigner residing among you, giving them food and clothing.
DEUTERONOMY 10:18 NIV

Since we have trekked everywhere from the Amazon jungles to the Sahara Desert, Renée and I have been the foreigners at scores of meals. We have enjoyed the generosity and good humor of our hosts, and sometimes had the meal of our lives. Other times? Well, let's just say the Bible says to eat whatever is put before you with thanksgiving. . .perhaps with an earnest prayer that you don't get sick!

Back home in the States, we have eaten with foreigners studying at a local university, and often found their food to be delicious. When we invite them to our home, we ask a few questions ahead of time so as to best serve them. Their dietary preferences and restrictions aren't right or wrong, just different.

And then there are the impoverished immigrants, often working two or three jobs to make do. They need a friend like you. Invite them over as well, and accept their invitations in return. Discover what they need, and do what you can to help. Always, the greater blessing is yours.

Lord, You've always had a great love for foreigners. I thank You that so many want an American friend. Make me one.

DATE: ....

Lord, I'm glad that hospitality is an expected part of each Christian's character and way of life. Please make it a bigger, more exciting part of my life in the coming days.

5 TOPICS COVERED THIS WEEK:

MONDAY: host your pastor for dinner
TUESDAY: host a missionary for dinner
WEDNESDAY: invite the poor
THURSDAY: host a disabled person
FRIDAY: host an immigrant for dinner

3 WAYS HOSPITALITY EXCITES ME:

1 ....

2 ....

3 ....

3 WAYS HOSPITALITY SCARES ME:

1 ....

2 ....

3 ....

How I want to respond to these truths:

....

....

....

....

....

....

....

....

LORD, HERE'S WHAT'S GOING ON IN MY LIFE RIGHT NOW. . .

OTHER THINGS I NEED TO SHARE WITH YOU, LORD. . .

Lord, when it comes to this new life map, I need to. . .

And do not forget to do good and to share with others, for with such sacrifices God is pleased.

HEBREWS 13:16 NIV

Thank You, Lord, for hearing my prayers and for helping me take action!

AMEN.

WEEK 11

BIBLE MEMORIZATION

The secret of memorizing anything is *loving* it. For example, my good friend Kevin has memorized the handwritten signatures of many great major league baseball players over the decades.

I love the Bible! And after I read it cover to cover, I started a second habit: memorizing one of the psalms each week. After committing fifty to memory, I switched over to memorizing New Testament passages from Romans to Jude. Two years later, Renée started doing the same thing.

Scripture memorization isn't a modern idea. It's what Joshua, David, Jeremiah, Daniel, Ezra, Paul, and other great men of God did in biblical times. They wrote down what God told them to write, but they also read and studied and learned what God had told other biblical writers too.

This week, I invite you to memorize five of the most famous and power-packed Bible passages given to us through Moses, David, John, and Paul.

To remember, learn to love!

I will delight in your statutes; I will not forget your word.

Psalm 119:16 ESV

MONDAY

MEMORIZE DEUTERONOMY 10:12–13

What does the LORD your God ask of you but to fear the LORD your God, to walk in obedience to him, to love him, to serve the LORD your God with all your heart and with all your soul, and to observe the LORD's commands and decrees that I am giving you today for your own good?
DEUTERONOMY 10:12–13 NIV

I love these two verses! Moses begins by asking a very important question. The operative conjunction is the word *but*. Moses then presents five very important answers:

1. "fear the LORD your God"
2. "walk in obedience to him"
3. "love him"
4. "serve the LORD your God with all your heart and with all your soul"
5. "observe the LORD's commands and decrees that I am giving you today for your own good"

Each of these five very important answers reverberates throughout the rest of the Bible. So learn and love them well.

Lord, help me right now to memorize these verses. I thank You for calling me to say yes to You. I do!

TUESDAY

MEMORIZE PSALM 23:1–6

The LORD is my shepherd, I lack nothing. He makes me lie down in green pastures, he leads me beside quiet waters, he refreshes my soul. He guides me along the right paths for his name's sake. Even though I walk through the darkest valley, I will fear no evil, for you are with me; your rod and your staff, they comfort me. You prepare a table before me in the presence of my enemies. You anoint my head with oil; my cup overflows. Surely your goodness and love will follow me all the days of my life, and I will dwell in the house of the LORD forever.

PSALM 23:1–6 NIV

Tens of millions have memorized the most famous of the 150 psalms, and for good reason. It doesn't matter which Bible translation you use. . .Psalm 23 is always powerful. In this psalm, David draws upon his years of experience as a shepherd to praise the Lord in picturesque, poignant, and poetic language. Specifically, David praises God for His (1) provision; (2) refreshment; (3) guidance; (4) protection and comfort; (5) anointing and joy; (6) goodness and love; and (7) promise of heaven.

Could you use some of those realities today? Memorize this psalm and refer to it often.

Lord, please help me to memorize Psalm 23 today. I praise You for Your many benefits and blessings in my own life.

WEDNESDAY

MEMORIZE JOHN 3:16–18

"For God so loved the world that he gave his one and only Son, that whoever believes in him shall not perish but have eternal life. For God did not send his Son into the world to condemn the world, but to save the world through him. Whoever believes in him is not condemned, but whoever does not believe stands condemned already because they have not believed in the name of God's one and only Son."

JOHN 3:16–18 NIV

Countless millions of children have memorized the most popular Bible verse of all, John 3:16. What's not to love about this winsome gospel sentence?

As adults, we would do well to memorize the apostle John's next two verses as well. Verse 17 affirms God's intention: to save us, not condemn us. Verse 18 confirms a choice each of us must make: to believe in Jesus (who He is, what He did for us) or not to believe (and stand condemned by the Judge of all the earth).

That last part may sound harsh, and it is. But how good to clearly know the choice before us. That way, no one need worry or fret—which is in keeping with the Lord's heart of love. He doesn't want *anyone* to perish. (If you want a very clear statement of that, look at 2 Peter 3:9.)

Lord, I thank You for Your heart of love.
It is amazing—may I enjoy it and share it.

THURSDAY

MEMORIZE ROMANS 10:9–10

If you openly declare that Jesus is Lord and believe in your heart that God raised him from the dead, you will be saved. For it is by believing in your heart that you are made right with God, and it is by openly declaring your faith that you are saved.

ROMANS 10:9–10 NLT

We can't memorize too many gospel verses, and these two have been favorites of D. L. Moody, Billy Graham, Luis Palau, and other great evangelists—as well as hundreds of thousands of youth and children's workers. Both verses are simple enough for students to grasp and deep enough for theologians to ponder.

Some translations use the words *confess* or *profess*, which are accurate, but the New Living Translation's phrasing of "openly declare" clearly conveys the apostle Paul's intent to today's readers. Here's an obvious question: In church, in small groups, in personal conversations, and on social media do *we* openly declare that Jesus is our Lord, Master, and King?

To be saved is to openly declare our trust in—and allegiance to—the Lord Jesus Christ, God's Son and our Savior. By memorizing this passage, you'll never forget that important fact.

Lord, thank You for making the way so clear. I'm so glad to openly declare my allegiance to You!

FRIDAY

MEMORIZE PHILIPPIANS 4:6–7

Don't worry about anything; instead, pray about everything.
Tell God what you need, and thank him for all he has done.
Then you will experience God's peace, which exceeds
anything we can understand. His peace will guard
your hearts and minds as you live in Christ Jesus.

PHILIPPIANS 4:6–7 NLT

This is my go-to scripture when I'm undergoing medical tests or other I-can't-proceed-yet experiences. Nothing calms my mind, relaxes my muscles, slows my heartbeat, and paces my breathing as quickly as the mental recitation of these two verses.

Full disclosure: I actually recite Philippians 4:4–9, 4:13, and 4:19. . .several times! I especially love verse 6, which contains four commands: (1) "Don't worry about anything"; (2) "pray about everything"; (3) "tell God what you need"; and (4) "thank him for all he has done."

Obeying these commands defines much of what it means to "live in Christ Jesus" (end of verse 7) and qualifies us to experience God's unsurpassed, protective peace in our hearts and minds (rest of verse 7). What could be better information to file deeply into your mind and heart?

Lord, Your commands and promises are my comfort,
solace, encouragement, strength, joy, and peace.
Help me always to live according to Your Word.

DATE: ....

Lord, I'm so glad that the secret to memorizing anything is delighting in it. As I memorize and review key verses of scripture, increase my love for and delight in You.

5 TOPICS COVERED THIS WEEK:

MONDAY: memorize Deuteronomy 10:12–13

TUESDAY: memorize Psalm 23:1–6

WEDNESDAY: memorize John 3:16–18

THURSDAY: memorize Romans 10:9–10

FRIDAY: memorize Philippians 4:6–7

3 WAYS MEMORIZING SCRIPTURE DELIGHTS ME:

1 ....

2 ....

3 ....

3 WAYS MEMORIZATION FRUSTRATES ME:

1 ....

2 ....

3 ....

How I want to respond to these truths:

....

....

....

....

....

....

....

....

LORD, HERE'S WHAT'S GOING ON IN MY LIFE RIGHT NOW. . .

OTHER THINGS I NEED TO SHARE WITH YOU, LORD. . .

Lord, when it comes to this new life map, I need to. . .

"I am the vine; you are the branches. If you remain in me and I in you, you will bear much fruit; apart from me you can do nothing."

JOHN 15:5 NIV

Thank You, Lord, for hearing my prayers and for helping me take action!

AMEN.

WEEK 12

GOD'S WILL, THE GENERAL ISSUES

In the Bible we sometimes find God telling Noah, Abraham, Joseph, Joshua, and other main characters what to do. Sometimes God spoke to them in person, at other times in dreams, and occasionally through other means. Yet each man knew, deep in his heart, that the Lord was with him and was directing his steps.

Imagine God speaking to you. It might be only once every few years, but when it does happen, you know it. One time, I begged God to tell me why our church's terrific youth pastor had suddenly quit coming to work. God answered, and I called the young man to invite him to lunch the next day. After we ordered, I told him what God said. He wept for five minutes.

But it's rare for God to speak to us so directly. That's why it's so important to know and apply key biblical principles about His will. This week, we will explore five such principles rooted in scripture.

He has told you, O man, what is good; and what does the LORD require of you but to do justice, and to love kindness, and to walk humbly with your God?

MICAH 6:8 ESV

MONDAY

GOD'S WILL IS BIG

"This, then, is how you should pray: 'Our Father in heaven, hallowed be your name, your kingdom come, your will be done, on earth as it is in heaven.'"

MATTHEW 6:9–10 NIV

God's will is bigger than we could ever dream. Years ago, Renée and I had such noble plans for her to finish college and then for us to go to the mission field. We were committed to serving God and eager to get where we wanted to go.

But God had different plans.

God wanted to teach me that He is more concerned with *how* we serve than *where* we serve, with *who we are* than *what we do*.

A wise mentor told us, "Your life is like a pump in the middle of a barnyard, isn't it? Anyone can get to you at any time. The minute you see them coming, you know they want something. . .and they expect you to deliver. You feel handled, don't you? Used. And that's good, isn't it? You want to be God's servant, so of course everyone who walks by is going to pump you. Your only problem is that your pipe isn't deep enough."

Lord, may my pipe go deep into Your nourishing love. Fill up my reservoirs so that I am satisfied, and then can pour out love to others.

TUESDAY

GOD'S WILL IS MUNDANE

"But seek first [God's] kingdom and his righteousness, and all these things will be given to you as well."
MATTHEW 6:33 NIV

God's will is more mundane than we would ever guess. Therefore, no man is above housework.

Around my place, two things reign supreme—dishes and laundry. Doing the dishes is relaxing, but folding clean laundry. . .I can see life there. Something about taking clean clothes from the basket and grouping them into logical piles does my heart good. A transformation from disorder to order—there's a promise and a sense of accomplishment.

Orderly piles of clean laundry give me a taste of what I'd relish in the rest of my life. Of course, the human beings who generate the content of those piles also help to create the hecticness that keeps my life spinning happily. So I enjoy my islands of order when I can, allowing them to spur me on to accomplish other mundane tasks.

Brother Lawrence, the seventeenth-century monk who wrote *The Practice of the Presence of God*, once said, "We ought not to be weary of doing little things for the love of God, who regards not the greatness of the work, but the love with which it is performed."

Lord, You know there are household jobs that I hate. But You are in every task, no matter how mundane. Therefore, I will do each one for You.

WEDNESDAY

GOD'S WILL IS HARD TO UNDERSTAND

And we know that in all things God works for the good of those who love him, who have been called according to his purpose.
ROMANS 8:28 NIV

God's will is complex, harder to understand now than it is later.

My dad and brother can think three-dimensionally; they can build anything. Not me—I even took a class in architectural design but could never get that third axis down. Someday, in the new heavens and new earth, I figure my glorified body, soul, and mind will get me up to three dimensions—though other people may be thinking six-dimensionally by then!

Like most men, I want to understand things—and quickly. When it comes to addition and multiplication, no problem. When it comes to advanced calculus and astrophysics, *big* problem. That doesn't mean the latter fall outside of God's perfect will. I just have to take their existence and applications by faith.

When the Lord called Joshua to march around Jericho for seven days, He didn't explain why. God simply said that He was the supreme commander and ordered Joshua to remove his sandals. Ordinary sand can become holy ground. Joshua obeyed what he knew and accomplished great things. So can we.

Lord, how often I want to understand Your will. But I also know You are growing my faith.

THURSDAY

GOD'S WILL IS LESS EXCITING

You need to persevere so that when you have done the will of God, you will receive what he has promised.
HEBREWS 10:36 NIV

God's will is sometimes less exciting than we might wish. Consider one man's story:

War had broken out, and the future of nations was at stake. Huge shipments of bullets arrived daily in a certain lab, where one specimen from each load was tested to ensure quality.

The man in charge of the testing couldn't have been more qualified for the job—he was a true master. But a burning patriotism fueled the man's desire to be on the front lines of the war effort. Finally, he received his orders, said farewell to his staff (including one of my wife's mentors), and went to the battle zone. And within a short time, he was gunned down by the enemy.

How tragic that this man couldn't see the tremendous significance of his behind-the-scenes contributions to the war effort.

Most of God's will is less than exciting. Of course, that's true of many of our responsibilities—on the job, at church, or in our home. But God doesn't call us to pursue what's thrilling. He calls us to persevere in doing His will.

Lord, help me to persevere in what You want me to do.

FRIDAY

GOD'S WILL TAKES LONGER

Now may the God of peace. . .equip you with everything good for doing his will, and may he work in us what is pleasing to him, through Jesus Christ, to whom be glory for ever and ever. Amen.

HEBREWS 13:20–21 NIV

God's will often takes much longer than we expect. Sadly, most men fail in God's waiting rooms. Why? There are several reasons.

First, many of us keep our eyes on other people. Key question: "What difference would it make if I didn't care what everyone else thought?"

Second, most men keep their eyes on their own expectations. Two realities: My expectations determine my length of obedience; therefore, I need to embrace *God's* expectations. My own expectations may be frustrated, but my growth doesn't need to be stunted.

Third, most men keep their eyes on the problem. Unlike King Saul, his son Jonathan had simple confidence in the reality of the God he served (see 1 Samuel 14). May we do the same.

Fourth, most men rationalize when they get up and walk out of God's waiting room. Instead, let's truly seek God's will day in and day out. Let's maintain an eternal perspective. After all, we have a very long time to celebrate our victories.

Lord, it's hard to wait—even at a stoplight. From now on, I want to embrace waiting. Help me!

Lord, I'm glad that You don't call me to pursue everything that's exciting and thrilling. Instead, You simply want me to persevere in doing Your will. That is my daily objective and goal.

5 TOPICS COVERED THIS WEEK:

MONDAY: God's will is big
TUESDAY: God's will is mundane
WEDNESDAY: God's will is hard to understand
THURSDAY: God's will is less exciting
FRIDAY: God's will takes longer

3 WAYS GOD'S WILL REWARDS ME:

1

2

3

3 WAYS GOD'S WILL ELUDES ME:

1

2

3

How I want to respond to these truths:

LORD, HERE'S WHAT'S GOING ON IN MY LIFE RIGHT NOW. . .

OTHER THINGS I NEED TO SHARE WITH YOU, LORD. . .

Lord, when it comes to this new life map, I need to. . .

Moses did everything just as the LORD commanded him.

EXODUS 40:16 NIV

Thank You, Lord, for hearing my prayers and for helping me take action!

AMEN.

WEEK 13

GOD'S WILL, THE SPECIFIC ISSUES

God's will isn't merely a set of general principles. At key points in life, His will becomes specific. This week, we'll consider five important personal issues: marriage, children, career, finances, and aspirations. The latter concerns what we really want to do in life.

Of course, what we *want* and what we *get* aren't always the same. Some men want to marry, but deeply struggle with the question "Who should I marry?" Other men dream about launching into specific careers, only to see doors repeatedly close.

One of my mentors reminded me, "David, you'll always *over*estimate what you can do in a year and *under*estimate what you can do in five"—let alone a lifetime. By the time I'd reached my fifties, I could tell Renée, "I've enjoyed life more than most. There is nothing more in my career that I need to prove. I want to stick around a long time, but I'm ready to die happy."

As in all of life, our focus needs to stay on the Lord God, creator of heaven and earth, who knows the end from the beginning. . .and who walks with us each step of the way between now and glory.

"Your [God the Father's] kingdom come,
your will be done, on earth as it is in heaven."
MATTHEW 6:10 NIV

MONDAY

GOD'S WILL: MARRIAGE

"If you do marry, you have not sinned."
1 Corinthians 7:28 NIV

By age thirteen I was convinced I would be celibate for life—this immediately after my crush had brushed me off like a stray piece of popcorn. By age seventeen I was convinced I wanted to delay dating Renée until after college. By age twenty-one I was convinced I should marry her immediately after graduation. What a difference four years can make!

When our children reached adolescence, Renée and I were quick to tell them that what we did was *not* the model for what they should do. Two of them followed it anyway. Three of them didn't. The model isn't what's right or wrong—instead, we focused on two commitments.

First, we encouraged our children to skip looking for the right person, and instead *become* the right person. Even more importantly, we strongly urged them to date and marry someone only if that person loved the Lord deeply and was committed to lifelong personal growth and maturity. "After all," we said, "you can work through any marriage problems if you're both willing to grow."

Lord, thank You for marriage. Please show me how to thrive in mine for years to come.

TUESDAY

GOD'S WILL: CHILDREN

Children are a gift from the Lord; they are a reward from him.

Psalm 127:3 NLT

Children are a gift from the Lord, but not for everyone. One of our daughters announced that she would never have kids, but her husband-to-be helped change her mind over time. After they were married, she wanted three kids and he wanted four. They compromised at three. . .with the possibility of adoption.

Personally, I had rigorously shaken my head *no* after accidentally overhearing Renée tell a friend that she wanted *eleven* children. After the birth of our first, Renée herself announced that was it—no more kids! Of course, these are momentary human emotions, not God's will. Renée and I decided on three kids, and ended up with five. We enjoy God's sense of humor.

As a couple we were blessed always to have another couple nearby who loved our children and frequently offered to care for them. Those sanity breaks made a huge difference for Renée and me. We later encouraged our children to consider living near in-laws; happy grandparents offer the sanity breaks that every young couple can use.

Children are a lot of work and expense, but they are always "a gift from the Lord. . .a reward from him." Whether you've had children or are hoping to, trust God to give you the family *He* has planned.

Lord, I need to trust You with everything, but especially issues as large and important as family. Guide me, I pray.

WEDNESDAY

GOD'S WILL: CAREER

Instead, you ought to say, "If it is the Lord's will, we will live and do this or that."
JAMES 4:15 NIV

My wife dreamed of being a writer. As a girl, Renée hoped to write and publish children's novels. She hasn't written any fiction yet, but God has given her more publishing opportunities than she ever dreamed possible.

What's more, Renée didn't pursue social work, but God moved her heart and then opened a door. She looks back now and sees how He wisely prepared her for this career on the frontlines working with foster children.

Not surprisingly, God pointed me in the right direction as well. Of course, for a few years it felt like the Lord was changing the channel a lot! News writing. Magazine editing. Book editing. Promoting large events. Social networking. The Lord orchestrated each step and then gave me a dream career at the busy intersection of all my previous work.

The best career advice? Pray, work hard, and watch for the opportunities God unveils.

**Lord, I'm willing to pray and work hard.
Please guide and provide.**

THURSDAY

GOD'S WILL: FINANCES

"The Lord gave and the Lord has taken away; may the name of the Lord be praised."
Job 1:21 NIV

While poor as church mice when we married, Renée and I were no strangers to hard work. I remember the quiet exuberance I felt when our assets reached a nice round figure, then doubled, then tripled. Our financial charts promised more of the same—or so I thought.

But without warning, our little company's largest clients pulled more than three hundred thousand dollars of work out from under us. This was many months before someone coined the term "Great Recession." Our asset pie chart flipped through the air and landed with a big *splat*. Our once-successful business failed, we went through bankruptcy, we lost our house. . .and Renée and I found ourselves once again as poor as church mice.

Is it wrong to have financial goals? No, definitely not. But we do need to hold everything with open hands. After losing his immense wealth, "Job did not sin by charging God with wrongdoing" (Job 1:22 NIV). In time, God doubly restored Job's fortune.

That's not guaranteed for anyone, of course. But why rail against God instead of seeking new financial blessings? Trust Him to provide for your needs, and pray and work toward the additional.

**Lord, I hold everything with open hands.
May Your name be praised.**

FRIDAY

GOD'S WILL: ASPIRATIONS

Let God transform you into a new person by changing the way you think. Then you will learn to know God's will for you, which is good and pleasing and perfect.
ROMANS 12:2 NLT

Let's go beyond career and financial goals today. In the rest of life, what do you *really* want to do? "I don't know," you might be thinking. "What else is there?" Here are several ideas:

First Tier: (1) Become a man who loves God wholeheartedly. (2) Become a man who loves others well. (3) Become a man of good character. (4) Become a man of goodwill in your community. (5) Become a leader in your church.

Second Tier: (6) Become a man of good humor. (7) Become a man who loves children well. (8) Become a man who tells stories about his most embarrassing failures. (9) Become a man who asks others, "What is your (life) story?" (10) Become a man who invites others to church.

Third Tier: (11) Become a lifelong reader of good books. (12) Become a lifelong learner of God's wisdom.

Lord, I thank You for giving me so many opportunities to pursue. Show me who You want me to be.

DATE:

Lord, my focus needs to stay on You for the rest of my life. After all, You know the end from the beginning, and You promise to walk with me each step of the way.

5 TOPICS COVERED THIS WEEK:

MONDAY: God's will: marriage
TUESDAY: God's will: children
WEDNESDAY: God's will: career
THURSDAY: God's will: finances
FRIDAY: God's will: aspirations

3 WAYS GOD'S WILL IS CLEAR TO ME:

1 ....

2 ....

3 ....

3 WAYS GOD'S WILL IS A MYSTERY TO ME:

1 ....

2 ....

3 ....

How I want to respond to these truths:

....

....

....

....

....

....

....

....

LORD, HERE'S WHAT'S GOING ON IN MY LIFE RIGHT NOW. . .

OTHER THINGS I NEED TO SHARE WITH YOU, LORD. . .

Lord, when it comes to this new life map, I need to. . .

Who, then, are those who fear the LORD? He will instruct them in the ways they should choose.

PSALM 25:12 NIV

Thank You, Lord, for hearing my prayers and for helping me take action!

AMEN.

WEEK 14

WORK, PART 1

This week, we're going to look at the world of work with some expert help from some friends of mine. Several are former Fortune 500 executives and consultants. Several others provide in-depth counseling to men at every career stage. They're quite a diverse group with some great things to teach us.

Some men bristle at the idea that anyone else has something to teach them. But when we think that way, we're choosing the pathway of mediocrity and eventual failure. Why would any man do such a thing? The answer is easy: stubborn pride.

The wise man seeks to grow in the Lord and in every major sphere of life—including his work. After all, work is where we invest the bulk of our waking hours each week. The average man works nearly a hundred thousand hours in his lifetime. Want to be successful? Then learn from the best.

This week, ask God to help you learn five key insights for success.

> *By the grace of God I am what I am, and his grace to me was not without effect. No, I worked harder than all of them—yet not I, but the grace of God that was with me.*
>
> 1 Corinthians 15:10 NIV

MONDAY

STRENGTH AND DEPENDENCE

The glory of young men is their strength,
gray hair the splendor of the old.
PROVERBS 20:29 NIV

I did it the hard way, but I finally learned I have two kinds of strengths.

Natural strengths are certain traits of personality that God gave me. If I operate within these strengths, I thrive. Conversely, if I try to convert a personal weakness into a strength, and then seek to operate out of this "learned" strength, I may thrive for a time—but then I crash, hard. Why? Because it takes so much work to operate out of the learned strengths, I either burn out or flee back to my natural strengths. Either way, what looked like a great start can become a huge mess.

One of my big goals is to operate out of my natural strengths, empowered by God, so that I can thrive. May you thrive too! Toward that end, I recommend that you read *Grace Revealed: Finding God's Strength in Any Crisis.* It's written by my good friend Fred Sievert, former president of New York Life Insurance. He's more successful—and dependent on God—than anyone else I know.

Lord, help me to know what strengths You gave me and to use them in dependence on You.

TUESDAY

DISQUIET AND DELIVERANCE

Why are you cast down, O my soul? And why are you disquieted within me? Hope in God; for I shall yet praise Him, the help of my countenance and my God.

PSALM 42:11 NKJV

A dedicated, successful, and hardworking leader told me about some serious problems within his organization. I asked: "Is it possible that your personal issues have colored or clouded your perceptions?" In this case, the answer, sadly, was a clear "yes."

A book I highly recommended that he read is *The Disquieted Soul.* It's written by a good friend, Lane Cohee, a former executive in the defense and aerospace sector.

"For as long as I can remember," Lane writes, "I have lived with a decidedly disquieted soul—a soul perpetually fueled by flames of anxiety and discontent. Over the years I rarely gave it serious thought, assuming that there were many more important matters in life. There are not." Lane adds: "In my experience, nothing is more important to recognize and remedy because, left unchecked, a disquieted soul is spiritually suicidal by nature. *It ultimately charts a path of its own undoing*" (emphasis his).

How is your soul at home? At work? At rest? In times of disquiet, what is the psalm writer's remedy?

Lord, I feel disquieted right now. Change my perceptions. Turn my gaze toward You. Be my joy and peace.

WEDNESDAY

QUESTIONS AND WISDOM

When the queen of Sheba heard about the fame of Solomon and his relationship to the Lord, she came to test Solomon with hard questions.

1 Kings 10:1 NIV

Each day this week I'm recommending a great book from the world of work. Today's is an e-book, *Leading with Questions.* It's written by my good friend Bob Tiede, who has trained untold thousands how to ask the right questions and pursue the right answers.

Bob writes: "Jesus did two things exceedingly well: He told great stories and He asked great questions." Of course, Jesus' stories always provoked questions, so He must have *loved* questions!

Thanks to Bob, I've thought a lot about Jesus and questions. Like you, I've heard people ask, "Is Jesus Lord of your life?" He *is*, now and for eternity. The better question is, "Have you acknowledged that fact?" How good it is to gladly acknowledge the Lord's place in the universe—and in your life and mine—here and now.

How does this apply to your work? If the entire universe was created through Jesus (Colossians 1:16), then He certainly knows your best fit in a job and career. Be sure to ask Him about it.

Lord, I gladly acknowledge You as Lord of my life. Any other response is unworthy of You and unfitting for the man You've made me to be.

THURSDAY

LOVE FOR GOD, OTHERS, SELF

"The second is this: 'Love your neighbor as yourself.' There is no commandment greater than these."
MARK 12:31 NIV

I've learned that every Christian needs to ask three probing questions. I only wish I had known these questions a few years ago: (1) Do I understand the greatest commandment and take it seriously? (2) Do I understand that I can love God wholeheartedly *only* if I have received, embraced, and cherished His deep love for me? (3) Do I understand that I can love my neighbors as myself *only* if I love myself?

If you're missing that final point, then the greatest commandment is mere theory. Granted, you may be working hard. Your work may astound others. But let's not kid ourselves—you're not fully engaged with others or yourself.

To become fully engaged, I recommend you read *The Missing Commandment: Love Yourself* by my good friends Jerry and Denise Basel, who lead a counseling ministry north of Atlanta. Their teaching resolved a deep, nagging question in my own life: What does it mean for me to obey Jesus and love others "as yourself"? It may help you just as much as it helped me.

Lord, thank You for speaking to my own heart. May I listen intently.

FRIDAY

ANGER AND TRUE REPENTANCE

But now you must also rid yourselves of all such things as these: anger, rage, malice, slander, and filthy language from your lips.

COLOSSIANS 3:8 NIV

If there's anything worse than uncontrolled anger in the workplace, it's uncontrolled anger at home. If you struggle with anger, I recommend *Confessions of an Angry Man*. It's written by my good friend Brent Hofer.

Brent writes: "Despite the truth that I had driven my wife to reject me, I knew a more important truth: God loved me. And He had the ability to transform the world that I had ruined. The gospel was true, after all!

"I came to believe that God was working for my good. He didn't want me angry and dominating my wife and children. He wanted me changed and He had not given up on me. My life was not over and I was not alone in the dark."

Brent found that his wife would be the key God used to unlock the shackles of his anger. God often uses the people closest to us—our family, our friends, our coworkers—to get our attention, *as long as we're willing to listen*. Has anyone been trying to get a message through to you lately?

Lord, give me ears to listen—to Your Word and to the loving people You've put in my life.

Lord, the wise man seeks to grow in You and in every major sphere of life—including work. After all, work is where I invest the bulk of my waking hours each week.

5 TOPICS COVERED THIS WEEK:

MONDAY: strength and dependence
TUESDAY: disquiet and deliverance
WEDNESDAY: questions and wisdom
THURSDAY: love for God, others, self
FRIDAY: anger and true repentance

3 WAYS LEARNING FROM OTHERS EMPOWERS ME:

1 ....

2 ....

3 ....

3 WAYS LEARNING FROM OTHERS FRUSTRATES ME:

1 ....

2 ....

3 ....

How I want to respond to these truths:

....

....

....

....

....

....

....

LORD, HERE'S WHAT'S GOING ON IN MY LIFE RIGHT NOW. . .

OTHER THINGS I NEED TO SHARE WITH YOU, LORD. . .

Lord, when it comes to this new life map, I need to. . .

Whatever you have learned or received or heard from me, or seen in me—put it into practice.

PHILIPPIANS 4:9 NIV

Thank You, Lord, for hearing my prayers and for helping me take action!

AMEN.

WEEK 15

WORK, PART 2

This week, ask God to help you learn five more key insights for success in the workplace. We have expert help again from some Fortune 500 executives and consultants. Others are experts in the worlds of sports memorabilia, biblical tourism, and investment and entrepreneurship. Again, it's quite a diverse group with some great things to teach us.

But even better than what they know and have done, these men exemplify life mapping at its best. This week we'll learn how to recognize your worth at work, and then find work that's a joy, work that feels like home, work that challenges, and work that wins both now and in the future.

If you were to have coffee with our first expert, he would be quick to say it's never too late to life-map the rest of your career. But don't emphasize *where* you're going to work—focus on the *kind of man* you're going to be.

> ***My son, do not forget my teaching, but let your heart keep my commandments, for length of days and years of life and peace they will add to you. Let not steadfast love and faithfulness forsake you; bind them around your neck; write them on the tablet of your heart. So you will find favor and good success in the sight of God and man.***
>
> **PROVERBS 3:1–4 ESV**

MONDAY

RECOGNIZE YOUR WORTH AT WORK

May the Lord our God show us his approval and make our efforts successful. Yes, make our efforts successful!
PSALM 90:17 NLT

Success is a funny word. It can indicate doing whatever it takes to climb your way to the top. It can also mean recognizing your worth at work based on what *God* says about who you are and what you're supposed to do.

"Once you understand the *why* behind work, you'll be able to pursue your career with confidence, embrace change, and approach your job with a whole heart—one that is fully submitted to God and ready for what He's called you to do. That's what makes work worth doing."

That's a quote from my good friend Tom Heetderks and his excellent book, *Work Worth Doing*. I especially love his seven Smart-with-Heart Actions, which emphasize the key verse 1 Samuel 16:7 (NIV): "The LORD does not look at the things people look at. People look at the outward appearance, but the LORD looks at the heart."

Imagine God both filling your heart and smiling as you work. It's possible every day!

Lord, I thank You for making Your home in me, for working in me. Please help me to feel Your approval and recognize my God-given worth on the job.

TUESDAY

WORK THAT'S A JOY

Whatever your hand finds to do, do it with all your might.
ECCLESIASTES 9:10 NIV

When we were kids, everyone asked, "What are you going to do when you grow up?" Interestingly, experts now say what we loved to do as boys is usually one of the top three indicators of our best career choices.

That's true in my own experience. When I was a kid, I loved sports, fishing, and the great outdoors. At age nine, I had the opportunity to serve as a writer and associate editor for a children's encyclopedia. Everything else was suddenly eclipsed by the fun and fascinating world of publishing.

That same year, 1969, my good friend Kevin Keating started collecting autographs from major league ballplayers. In his book *Waiting for a Sign*, Kevin says he would stand outside a stadium for an hour before the players arrived, hoping to snag a signature. Today, he's a premier autograph authenticator for collectors around the world.

What did *you* love doing as a kid? What might that indicate about work you could enjoy?

Lord, I want my work to align with the skills and passions You've given me. Please help me to find wise counsel and work that's a joy.

WEDNESDAY

WORK THAT FEELS LIKE HOME

Jesus said, "Come to me, all of you who are weary and carry heavy burdens, and I will give you rest."
MATTHEW 11:28 NLT

Growing up, I lived in two places and three houses. The second house was on the east end of a large island off mainland Alaska. The other two houses were located on the north end of Seattle. Guess which place was my favorite?

My good friend Andre Moubarak was born into a Christian family along the Via Dolorosa in Old Jerusalem's Christian Quarter. He begins his book *One Friday in Jerusalem* by describing how he played on the Way of Sorrow's ancient stones. Its winding pathway and sites "are as familiar to me as your living room is to you." Today, Andre is an ordained minister and licensed tour guide who helps people see the Bible anew through Middle Eastern eyes.

Many guys move away for college, then move again for their first career job, and never return to their childhood roots. Andre was able to find work that feels like home. Does any part of his story resonate with you?

Lord, You know what's best for me and my family. Please guide me into the place that brings You glory—and me contentment.

THURSDAY

WORK THAT CHALLENGES

Do you see someone skilled in their work? They will serve before kings; they will not serve before officials of low rank.

PROVERBS 22:29 NIV

If you know you're going to live forever, what risks are you willing to take here on earth?

As a young man, I pulled off several life-threatening stunts, including glissading. None of those things were motivated by God, though. It's only by His grace that I lived long enough to get married. My good friend Curt Laird, however, was attracted to his future wife precisely because she (like he) is absolutely fearless.

Curt has worked in more than thirty countries. Among many achievements, he built successful businesses across war-torn Afghanistan—including a billion-dollar mobile phone company. In his book *The Culture Key*, Curt unpacks the underlying principles that govern business in these regions. I especially like his Belief Tool, which has many applications for those of us who live and work in the United States.

Your boss may never ask you to work overseas. . .though he could. Or what if your boss offered you a leadership training program? Or some other challenge that stretched you? Would you be willing to say yes? If so, God may use you in ways you never dreamed possible.

Lord, I'm willing to following Your leading anywhere.

FRIDAY

WORK THAT WINS

"In the same way, let your light shine before others, that they may see your good deeds and glorify your Father in heaven."
MATTHEW 5:16 NIV

Will your job even exist in five or ten years? My good friends Mitch Little and Hendre Coetzee doubt it. In their book *Shiftability*, they write: "We could almost say anyone in any business role today faces an uncertain future. We live in an age of disruption and disintermediation. The business landscape is rapidly and radically changing and it keeps getting harder to predict what lies ahead."

So what do you predict about your own job? Will it look the same in a few years? Will it be there at all? Should you be making shifts to your work mindset now? In other words, what limiting beliefs should you shed in order to successfully prepare for your future work?

Mitch and Hendre are both enthusiastic about the opportunities ahead. Keep that in mind as you fill out this weekend's life map. God has great plans for you.

Lord, I want to be open to changing how I think so that I'm ready for whatever happens to my work. Guide my career, I pray!

Lord, I want to recognize my worth at work based on what You say about who I am and what I'm supposed to do. Please fill my heart with Your wisdom and smile over my work.

5 TOPICS COVERED THIS WEEK:

MONDAY: recognize your worth at work
TUESDAY: work that's a joy
WEDNESDAY: work that feels like home
THURSDAY: work that challenges
FRIDAY: work that wins

3 WAYS THAT WORK BUILDS ME UP:

1 ....
2 ....
3 ....

3 WAYS THAT WORK GRINDS ME DOWN:

1 ....
2 ....
3 ....

How I want to respond to these truths:

LORD, HERE'S WHAT'S GOING ON IN MY LIFE RIGHT NOW. . .

OTHER THINGS I NEED TO SHARE WITH YOU, LORD. . .

Lord, when it comes to this new life map, I need to. . .

For God has not given us a spirit of fear and timidity, but of power, love, and self-discipline.

2 TIMOTHY 1:7 NLT

Thank You, Lord, for hearing my prayers and for helping me take action!

AMEN.

WEEK 16

REST

I used to adhere to the adage, "Work as if it all depends on you. Pray as if it all depends on God." It's one of those short, pithy sayings that has the ring of truth, but sadly falls short.

To my chagrin, I must confess that I was a workaholic for most of my career. I took that "work as if it all depends on you" idea far too seriously, putting in a lot of hours. Though I accomplished many good things, I never knew how to stop. Even on vacation, I found ways to fly off for a day to speak and teach and consult. . .then jot down new plans the minute I boarded the plane back to my family. Type A, anyone?

Finally, God broke my health, forcing me to slow down. In hindsight, it was one of the best things that ever happened to me. I sure wouldn't wish broken health on anyone else, but I deeply value God's wonderful gifts of earnest prayer and true rest that I learned when I was down.

Bottom line: It all depends on *God*. If we do His will, we can leave the rest in His hands.

"In returning and rest you shall be saved;
in quietness and in trust shall be your strength."
Isaiah 30:15 esv

MONDAY

START AND THEN STOP

In vain you rise early and stay up late, toiling for food to eat—for [the LORD] grants sleep to those he loves.
PSALM 127:2 NIV

If you talk with my wife or any of our children, they will quickly confirm that I never knew when work started or stopped. I was always "on." My focus was accomplishing as much as possible, to as high a degree of excellence as possible, as fast as possible. If I wasn't accomplishing something *right now*, I was brainstorming what else to pursue.

Now it is true that while on vacation or traveling overseas, I could stop working for a while to focus on the people and experiences at hand. But never for the full trip or vacation. Success wasn't enough. I wanted to be *hyper* successful. In the end, though, how much of what I planned and did really mattered? At best, maybe half.

These past few years, I've finally learned to identify when my work starts and when it stops. Even better? I've learned to shut off my work brain after hours. As much as humanly possible, I gladly enjoy the "rest" of my day.

How do you unplug after work? Is there an "after work"? Ask God to help you rest.

Lord, thank You for offering sleep to those You love. May I take advantage of it!

TUESDAY

POWER NAPS

You [the Lord] will keep in perfect peace those whose minds are steadfast, because they trust in you.
Isaiah 26:3 niv

One of my favorite mentors was a high school principal. I didn't attend his school, but he took me under his wing for a couple of years. He was a man of boundless energy, and one day he told me a secret: at a set time every day, he got up from his desk, got down on his office floor, and took a twenty-minute nap. His secretary guarded that time carefully.

"The secret is discipline," he told me. "Make it every day. The same time. Exactly twenty minutes. Never use an alarm. Instead, tell yourself to wake up automatically after exactly twenty minutes. Do that and you'll be a new man for the rest of the day."

Not every workplace allows for naps, but companies are becoming more progressive all the time. Is there anything you could do to build this kind of rest into your work schedule? (Just don't try it on public transportation. I nodded off one day and woke up halfway to the next city!)

Lord, I'd love to find more time to rest, but how? I pray for Your wisdom and leading.

WEDNESDAY

USE PAPER AND PEN

At this I awoke and looked around.
My sleep had been pleasant to me.
JEREMIAH 31:26 NIV

Before we take a power nap or drop off to sleep at night, our brains needle us with reminders of things we still need to do. For many of us, if we don't write each one down immediately, our brains just won't let us rest. That's why you'll find a pad of Post-its by my bed, and a note-to-self text message or two on my phone.

Why is it so important to write things down? First, because our brains are easily distracted. Second, because we're prone to forget, no matter how earnest we are.

The more we write down, the less we have to remember—and the less we need to worry. I like to quip that once I write something down, it's as good as done. No, I won't necessarily do that thing next, but I typically will do it that day. If it's not an immediate need, I set a specific date on the Google calendar I share with Renée.

Twenty seconds now makes all the difference between good intentions and real actions—and better sleep!

Lord, please help me to cultivate the habit of writing important things down. I want to save my mental energy for more important matters—like You!

THURSDAY

ENJOY GOOD NIGHTS OF SLEEP

I lie down and sleep; I wake again,
because the Lord sustains me.
Psalm 3:5 NIV

The Bible repeatedly describes men who had to work all night. The list includes Joshua and his army, Joab and his regiment, and Peter and his fishing crew. Others who stayed up all night were Moses, while talking with God, and David, who wept before God.

Until my mid-fifties, I could occasionally stay up all night while working, traveling, or caring for a sick child. If I try that now, I feel absolutely wretched by early afternoon the next day. As we get older, a full night's sleep sometimes becomes more of a challenge. . .but there are some tricks to improve your rest.

Going to bed at the same time every night helps our sleep. And so does keeping the bedroom's temperature a few degrees cooler than normal. Turn off all screens at least an hour before retiring, and make sure the television is in another room.

God made the human body to need rest. Don't short-circuit that good night's sleep He offers.

Lord, show me what I can do to enjoy good nights of sleep.

FRIDAY

SCHEDULE YOUR SABBATHS

[Jesus said,] "Come to me, all you who are weary and burdened, and I will give you rest."
MATTHEW 11:28 NIV

The devil likes to twist God's good gifts—whether art and music, the act of sex, or even our Sabbath days. A Sabbath is dedicated to doing something different from other periods of time. In the Bible, the Sabbath meant a day without work each week. Each Sabbath started early Friday evening and finished early Saturday evening. They were days of rest and worship and reflection, days typically spent in one's home or courtyard with a break to attend the synagogue.

A Sabbath rest is required by the Ten Commandments. But that's the only one of the Ten Commandments *not* repeated in the teachings of Jesus and His apostles. It's not that Sabbaths are obsolete, though. In our busy lives, they're more important than ever.

For many of us, Sunday is a good Sabbath day. But you can schedule one on another day of the week if your work schedule demands. Whatever day it is, prioritize rest and reflection. Include Bible reading, prayer, praise, and other forms of worship. You'll find that the exercise of the Sabbath brings rest.

Lord, which day should I choose for a Sabbath? What do You want me to do—and not do?

DATE:

Lord, help me to slow down when I'm tempted to work too hard, too long, and for too many ultimately unimportant reasons.

5 TOPICS COVERED THIS WEEK:

MONDAY: start and then stop
TUESDAY: power naps
WEDNESDAY: use paper and pen
THURSDAY: enjoy good nights of sleep
FRIDAY: schedule your Sabbaths

3 WAYS REST HELPS ME:

1. ...
2. ...
3. ...

3 WAYS REST CONCERNS ME:

1. ...
2. ...
3. ...

How I want to respond to these truths:

LORD, HERE'S WHAT'S GOING ON IN MY LIFE RIGHT NOW. . .

OTHER THINGS I NEED TO SHARE WITH YOU, LORD. . .

Lord, when it comes to this new life map, I need to. . .

May the God of hope fill you with all joy and peace in believing, so that by the power of the Holy Spirit you may abound in hope.

ROMANS 15:13 ESV

Thank You, Lord, for hearing my prayers and for helping me take action!

AMEN.

WEEK 17

RECREATION

God created humans to explore and discover and enjoy the world He made. But as finite beings, we can't just keep going. Just as we need rest, we also need restoration.

Recreational activities engage our minds and bodies in new ways, providing much-needed enjoyment. Recreation can happen anywhere, but getting outside in our very "inside" culture enables our minds and bodies to renew. Not surprisingly, practitioners of both physical and mental health recommend time in nature on a regular basis.

My wife's employer sends a monthly email encouraging "wonder walks" in nature to cultivate awe, the heightened awareness of beauty and mystery. How easy to walk in wonder when you already know the Creator and can fully enjoy all He has made.

This week, let's look at recreation in a new way—not just as another activity, but as a practice of refreshment. Let's explore how to re-create our minds, bodies, emotions, and spirits.

There is a time for everything, and a season for every activity under the heavens.
ECCLESIASTES 3:1 NIV

MONDAY

RE-CREATE OUTDOORS

O Lord, what a variety of things you have made!
In wisdom you have made them all.
Psalm 104:24 NLT

My friends Richard and Julie took their kids to the mountain to ride inner tubes. After a slow start (you have to buy tickets and use the bathroom, you know), they finally found the youth group whose activity they were joining. They were overdressed and soon sweating.

The hassles could have stressed out Julie in particular, but she found herself happy and invigorated. Not just by the fresh air but by visiting a unique and beautiful place as a family. She wondered, "Why haven't we done this before?"

As I write this devotional, I'm looking out over the Pacific Ocean. I come to the picturesque Oregon coast at least three times a year, and I always feel renewed by it. Sometimes Renée and I bring friends and enjoy games of boccie. We always enjoy time on the beach.

Now I'm wondering: How will I re-create the rest of the year? We'll consider that question together this week.

Lord, I thank You for the variety of ways
we can re-create outdoors.

TUESDAY

PLAN AHEAD SO YOU CAN PLAY

[Jesus] said to them, "Come with me by yourselves to a quiet place and get some rest."
MARK 6:31 NIV

Open your calendar today and schedule some days for recreation, even if you don't know what activities you'll do. If you don't set time aside for recreation, the days will fill up with other things. Planning ahead helps to ensure recreation happens—and provides opportunity for more time with the key people in your life.

Need ideas? Look up events in your community and consult your local parks and recreation website. Peruse the brochures at a nearby hotel for excursions and tours. Nature societies offer specialized hikes and learning experiences. Pretend you're a tourist and explore your own community! Take a day trip by car, bus, or train to a different city—or drive through the countryside, stopping at local fruit stands.

You can even ask your friends to include you in their recreational activities. When you're looking to improve your mental and emotional health, why not include the important people God's put into your life?

Lord, please help me to plan for recreation. I know I'll be happier and better able to represent You.

WEDNESDAY

FIND YOUR BEST FIT

[The LORD] satisfies your desires with good things so that your youth is renewed like the eagle's.

PSALM 103:5 NIV

Not every activity refreshes your body, soul, and spirit. Trying new things enriches you, but doing what you *love* rejuvenates you. What are your recovery needs? Something that slows your mind and body or something that gets your heart rate pumping? What about activities that allow you to lose track of time and let your creativity flow?

My wife's best days feature strolls through the steep woods up to the meadow atop the park near our home. When she fills her lungs with forest-scented air, her shoulders relax and her eyes are drawn up to the trees and the sky. Her mind settles down and her spirit praises God.

Our friends Troy and Jodie use wheelchairs and no longer drive, but they take the metro to attend street fairs, festivals, and outdoor concerts. Rex, Paul, and Matt love to get away from civilization in the deep wilderness. Other friends of mine love to hike, fish, and swim. Still others spend hours photographing nature.

What's your best fit? How might it refresh your spirit and point you to God?

Lord, I thank You that You're always ready to bless me physically, mentally, emotionally, and spiritually.

THURSDAY

PAY FOR YOUR PLAY

Whatever is good and perfect is a gift coming down to us from God our Father, who created all the lights in the heavens. He never changes or casts a shifting shadow.
JAMES 1:17 NLT

Budget for and invest in recreation. You might join a local rec team for a reasonable fee or get a pass to the nearest public swimming pool, YMCA, or state or national park.

My son-in-law grew up skiing, but that wasn't something we did with our kids. My daughter, though, eventually took a college elective to learn how to ski—and got engaged on a black diamond slope. Now she and her husband invest their time and money in biking with their young family.

If a particular activity becomes a favorite, consider making the investment into that. Those costs meet the real need of caring for yourself.

Whatever you enjoy doing, remember that it is a gift of God. And when you enjoy it with thanksgiving, it can be a form of worship!

Lord, I'm glad that You're the Lord of all of life—even of my recreation.

FRIDAY

ARE YOU HAVING FUN YET?

The Lord has compassion on those who fear him; for he knows how we are formed, he remembers that we are dust.

Psalm 103:13–14 niv

Some men don't take enough time to stop and play. Others suffer from FOMO—fear of missing out. And for every man anxious that he might be missing out on some fun, many more worry that their children are. Not much true recreation happens if the family calendar is so full that everyone is exhausted and cranky.

Our culture offers more amazing experiences than any one person could enjoy in a lifetime. Planning and pursuing recreation is well worth the time and effort, but every weekend doesn't have to feel like Disneyland.

How many activities can you or your family pursue in a season? Have you considered limiting the number of sports or other activities each child participates in? Have you thought about how much time *you* spend on your own activities?

Do you have too many or too few outings on your calendar? Why not sit down today and plan something—or cancel an activity or two—so you can truly experience the joy and refreshment of recreation.

Lord, I want to be refreshed and renewed, not just busy.

Lord, I thank You that recreational activities engage my mind and body in new ways, providing much-needed enjoyment and restoration.

5 TOPICS COVERED THIS WEEK:

MONDAY: re-create outdoors
TUESDAY: plan ahead so you can play
WEDNESDAY: find your best fit
THURSDAY: pay for your play
FRIDAY: are you having fun yet?

3 WAYS RECREATION RESTORES ME:

1 ...

2 ...

3 ...

3 WAYS RECREATION DEPLETES ME:

1 ...

2 ...

3 ...

How I want to respond to these truths:

LORD, HERE'S WHAT'S GOING ON IN MY LIFE RIGHT NOW...

OTHER THINGS I NEED TO SHARE WITH YOU, LORD...

Lord, when it comes to this new life map, I need to...

"My purpose is to give them a rich and satisfying life."

JOHN 10:10 NLT

Thank You, Lord, for hearing my prayers and for helping me take action!

AMEN.

WEEK 18

ENTERTAINMENT

This week we're going to focus on entertainment. Like you, I'm all for enjoying music, movies, television series, streaming libraries, and apps. My goal? To help you cultivate a new vision for the role of entertainment in your own life.

In our culture, entertainment is everywhere. It's almost impossible to avoid celebrities and athletes and their work. A lot of entertainment is great, either as a way to relax or to be challenged to see the world through new eyes. Some aspects of our entertainment culture, though, require some real discernment.

For the next week, we'll consider principles for approaching entertainment "Christianly." I hope these thoughts will inform your consumption of entertainment while giving you a greater love for the Lord.

Everything good is a gift from God to be enjoyed. I do hope you experience much joy this week!

Whether you eat or drink or whatever you do, do it all for the glory of God.
1 Corinthians 10:31 niv

MONDAY

THE BIG PICTURE

Finally, brothers and sisters, whatever is true,
whatever is noble, whatever is right, whatever is pure,
whatever is lovely, whatever is admirable—if anything is
excellent or praiseworthy—think about such things.

PHILIPPIANS 4:8 NIV

"The big picture" doesn't mean the latest blockbuster. Let's begin our week by discussing the very important principle of Philippians 4:8.

The apostle Paul's words here encapsulate and elaborate other teachings throughout scripture. Paul also wrote Romans 8:6 ("The mind governed by the flesh is death, but the mind governed by the Spirit is life and peace"), Ephesians 4:17 ("I tell you this, and insist on it in the Lord, that you must no longer live as the Gentiles do, in the futility of their thinking"), and 1 Corinthians 2:16 ("We have the mind of Christ"). And the psalms and proverbs contain many instructions on how to be wise and godly in our thoughts (for example, Psalm 1:2, 63:6, 77:12, 119:15, and 143:5).

The point is simply this: God wants us to engage our minds with Him and His truth. Some forms of entertainment will help us to do that. Others will be neutral, and some will actively oppose the Lord. This week, we'll consider ways of approaching and even redeeming our entertainment.

Lord, I want to fill my mind with good things.
Please guide me in my approach to entertainment.

TUESDAY

A CASE FOR ENTERTAINMENT

"As some of your own poets have said,
'We are his offspring.'"
ACTS 17:28 NIV

Depending on your age and church background, you may have been taught that many forms of entertainment were inappropriate for Christians. Attitudes are much more relaxed these days, but not too long ago, many churches frowned on attending movies. A century or more back, many leading preachers discouraged people from watching theater productions.

Personal convictions on such things are fine (see Romans 14). But it's interesting to note that the apostle Paul was very aware of the entertainment culture of his day. In the verse above, he quotes an Athenian poet; he may have quoted a centuries-old Greek play in 1 Corinthians 15:33; and several times he referenced the sporting events of his world (see 1 Corinthians 9:24, 26; Galatians 2:2, 5:7). Always, Paul used these examples to make some distinctly Christian points.

As you approach your entertainment options, why not do the same thing? Watch, listen, and experience with a goal of seeing Jesus more clearly. I'll have some suggestions for how to do that in the next two readings.

Lord, please help me to "see" Jesus today in my entertainment choices. What would You have me to enjoy?

WEDNESDAY

APPROACH ENTERTAINMENT THOUGHTFULLY

We use our powerful God-tools for smashing warped philosophies, tearing down barriers erected against the truth of God, fitting every loose thought and emotion and impulse into the structure of life shaped by Christ.

2 Corinthians 10:5 msg

We turn to entertainment to escape the troubles and frustrations of real life. There's a lot of value in that, but as Christians we help ourselves by keeping our brains (and spirits) engaged.

Some movies and music and other types of entertainment will support our love and worship of God—and by approaching these thoughtfully, we can learn even more about Him and the life we should live. Some forms of entertainment require more discernment—they represent the ways and values of our world, and a thoughtful approach is to filter their messages through scripture. For example, it may be exciting, from our human perspective, to see a mistreated movie character wreak revenge on the bad guy—but Romans 12:19 clearly says that is *God's* job, not ours.

As we consume entertainment, may we always be *thinking*—"fitting every loose thought and emotion and impulse into the structure of life shaped by Christ."

Lord, I'm thankful for the mind You've given me. Please keep it engaged with Your truth, even as I'm being entertained.

THURSDAY

BE AWARE OF THEMES

Discretion will protect you,
and understanding will guard you.
PROVERBS 2:11 NIV

Yesterday, I encouraged you to approach entertainment thoughtfully. Today, we'll build upon that idea.

One thing to note as you watch, listen, read, or play is the *theme* of the entertainment. What is the underlying message of the movie, song, book, or game? Many times, completely secular entertainments still emphasize Christian themes—of family, duty, forgiveness, hope, courage, love, you name it. That's to be expected, since God wrote the biggest and best story to begin with!

At other times, the themes are negative, nothing you'd want to build your life upon. Even in these cases, though, a thoughtful consideration of the underlying message can remind you of the incredible value of God's Word. Knowing His truth, you don't have to live the kind of hard life so often depicted in media.

Allow your entertainment choices to generate gratitude to God—either for their positive, uplifting messages or for the realization of what He has saved you from.

Lord, may I always appreciate the salvation
I have through Jesus—whether a particular
entertainment celebrates or dismisses it.

FRIDAY

A WORD OF WARNING

Guard your heart above all else,
for it determines the course of your life.
PROVERBS 4:23 NLT

I have offered a positive take on the issue of entertainment because I believe it's one of the many potentially good things God has given us to enjoy. But we need to be honest about its dangers too. Just as medicine or sex or even a fast car can be misused to our harm, so can movies, music, and other diversions.

They're called "diversions" because they divert our attention—and that's where the danger lies. As Christians, we should always keep the Lord in our thoughts. If binge-watching movies or television episodes crowds Him out, or if violence or profanity or sexual content dulls our minds to the teaching of Philippians 4:8, we're inviting danger into our lives. And that's not something we want on our life map!

God wants to be involved in every aspect of life, even our amusements. Ask Him for guidance, and He will gladly answer. Enjoy what He allows, and thank Him for the opportunity to rest and refresh through entertainment.

Lord, I'm grateful for the breaks You give me
from the stresses of life. Help me to honor
You through my entertainment choices.

DATE: ....

Lord, everything good is a gift from You to be enjoyed with thanksgiving. Help me to cultivate a vision for the role of entertainment in my life that glorifies You.

5 TOPICS COVERED THIS WEEK:

MONDAY: the big picture
TUESDAY: a case for entertainment
WEDNESDAY: approach entertainment thoughtfully
THURSDAY: be aware of themes
FRIDAY: a word of warning

3 WAYS ENTERTAINMENT INSPIRES ME:

1 ....

2 ....

3 ....

3 WAYS ENTERTAINMENT MAKES ME STUMBLE:

1 ....

2 ....

3 ....

How I want to respond to these truths:

....

....

....

....

....

....

....

....

LORD, HERE'S WHAT'S GOING ON IN MY LIFE RIGHT NOW. . .

OTHER THINGS I NEED TO SHARE WITH YOU, LORD. . .

Lord, when it comes to this new life map, I need to. . .

God. . .richly gives us all we need for our enjoyment.
1 TIMOTHY 6:17 NLT

Thank You, Lord, for hearing my prayers and for helping me take action!
AMEN.

WEEK 19

PERSONAL IMPROVEMENT

My favorite color? The evergreen of a stately tree against a brilliant blue sky. I find myself walking down the street noting each tree with a calculating eye. I cheer certain trees on, willing them to grow faster. If only I could make it so!

Often, I feel the same way about my own personal improvement, wishing it was like putting Miracle-Gro on the plants in a well-kept garden. "Just add prayer and Bible reading!"—and then spiritual, mental, and emotional growth will appear. It doesn't work that way, though. Like trees, human beings need a long time to mature.

I can't force personal growth on myself or anyone else. But I can pursue it. Through faithful dependence on our Source, Jesus Christ, I will begin to see the maturation I long for.

May this week's devotionals cheer you on as you depend evermore upon the Lord.

His delight is in the law of the Lord, and on his law he meditates day and night. He is like a tree planted by streams of water that yields its fruit in its season, and its leaf does not wither. In all that he does, he prospers.

Psalm 1:2–3 ESV

MONDAY

GROW SPIRITUALLY

So neither the one who plants nor the one who waters is anything, but only God, who makes things grow.
1 Corinthians 3:7 NIV

My wife, Renée, and I grow delicious honey raspberries. In Asia, they are commonly called yellow or golden Himalayan raspberries. Our master gardener friends think of them as *Rubus ellipticus*.

Near the end of winter, my first job is to trim all the vines back to twelve inches and then recycle everything I've just cut away. After that, rain, sunshine, and warm weather do the rest. By the Fourth of July, the vines often are six feet tall and full of berries for the rest of summer and the early weeks of autumn. When I share the honey raspberries with family and friends, who gets the credit? Not me—*God* makes things grow.

In the garden of my soul, God's first job is to trim back the branches and twigs. How I choose to experience that trimming is so important: Am I mourning my losses or anticipating growth? After that, how do I choose to experience the wind, rain, hail, clouds, and sunshine He sends? Do I see them all as God's good hand of blessing for my spiritual growth and fruitfulness?

Lord, many times I'd rather skip the trimming and go straight to growth. Please change my mindset to honor Your wise management of my life.

TUESDAY

GROW SOCIALLY

We ought always to give thanks to God for you, brothers, as is right, because your faith is growing abundantly, and the love of every one of you for one another is increasing.
2 THESSALONIANS 1:3 ESV

How many people do you know? Have a number in mind? Now quadruple it. The reality is that all of us have several spheres of relationships. You have immediate and extended family, but don't forget your distant relatives. You have immediate and secondary colleagues at work, but don't forget all those former colleagues down through the years. You have high school and college friends, but don't forget the teachers and professors and staff you got to know too.

Of course, we can only be close with a certain number of people. Here's an idea for deepening those relationships: Purchase some three-by-five-inch index cards. Use them to jot down prayer needs of specific family members and friends. Make a commitment to pray for each of them weekly. Then start casually mentioning, "I pray for you every week." Then ask, "How can I best pray for you these next couple of weeks?"

Nothing revolutionizes your social life more than intentional, heartfelt prayer for those who mean the most to you.

Lord, the apostle Paul highly valued prayer for others. May I do the same.

WEDNESDAY

GROW MENTALLY

Live a life worthy of the Lord and please him in every way: bearing fruit in every good work, growing in the knowledge of God.

Colossians 1:10 niv

Time magazine once published an article that indicated many people buy best-selling books without ever reading them. An accompanying chart named a dozen popular books and a best guess of how many people had actually read them. The estimates went as low as one percent!

In other words, it may be fashionable to have best-selling books on your coffee table, but we have no idea if you've read them. What's even worse for me? When someone gives me a tour of his home and I can't spot a single book anywhere. That implication is that this person devalues mental stimulation and growth. He's allowing his mind to atrophy.

Long gone are the days where every home had a family Bible. Yet reading God's Word, the holy scriptures, is what generates fear of the Lord and true wisdom (Job 28:28; Psalm 111:10; Proverbs 1:7, 2:5, 9:10; Ecclesiastes 12:12–14).

Read other good books, certainly. But never neglect the Book of books!

Lord, I thank You for giving us Your Word, which is more relevant now than ever.

THURSDAY

GROW EMOTIONALLY

Grow in the grace and knowledge of our Lord and Savior Jesus Christ. To him be glory both now and forever!
2 Peter 3:18 NIV

My good friend Jeannie Clarkson told me, "In my counseling practice, I work with lots of people experiencing overwhelming negative emotions—shame, fear, anxiety, or anger, for example—as we all do at times. Everyone, myself included, benefits when we grow in our ability to understand and manage our feelings."

We both highly recommend the book *Why Emotions Matter* by Tristen and Jonathan Collins, fellow Christian authors in my hometown of Portland, Oregon. Jeannie says, "Their book will definitely help if you find yourself struggling or being swept away by negative emotions. You will learn to recognize negative feelings before they get out of hand as well as increase your more positive happy feelings."

Most men (including me!) need to grow emotionally. Jonathan quips that he didn't even know he had emotions until he started going to marriage counseling with Tristen. Now they're growing and thriving, having a huge impact for God's glory. You can too!

**Lord, I know I need to grow emotionally.
Show me how to manage my feelings and honor You.**

FRIDAY

GROW VOLITIONALLY

It is God who works in you to will and to act in order to fulfill his good purpose.
PHILIPPIANS 2:13 NIV

If there's any area of life where we need to depend on the Lord fully and completely, it's in the area of growing *volitionally*. What does that mean? We all make hundreds of choices each day. God doesn't really care about the color of your socks. But He cares deeply about your choices for and against His written Word, the Bible. What's more, He cares deeply about your decisions for and against your "neighbors"—including your family and friends and colleagues.

Most decisions we make are benign. Beverage companies make it seem like a big deal, but what you drink with lunch probably won't register on the Richter scale. What you think about another person at lunch, or what you say to him, or *how* you say it—now those are the kinds of choices God watches.

Here are three ways to grow volitionally: (1) Don't sweat life's little decisions. (2) Do sweat how you impact others. (3) When you blow it, apologize.

Lord, remind me how my choices impact others—and my own heart. Change me from the inside out.

DATE: ....

Lord Jesus, personal improvement doesn't come overnight. Instead, it comes through faithful dependence on You, my Creator and Maker.

5 TOPICS COVERED THIS WEEK:

MONDAY: grow spiritually
TUESDAY: grow socially
WEDNESDAY: grow mentally
THURSDAY: grow emotionally
FRIDAY: grow volitionally

3 WAYS PERSONAL GROWTH EXCITES ME:

1 ....

2 ....

3 ....

3 WAYS PERSONAL GROWTH TROUBLES ME:

1 ....

2 ....

3 ....

How I want to respond to these truths:

....

....

....

....

....

....

....

....

LORD, HERE'S WHAT'S GOING ON IN MY LIFE RIGHT NOW. . .

OTHER THINGS I NEED TO SHARE WITH YOU, LORD. . .

Lord, when it comes to this new life map, I need to. . .

I press on toward the goal to win the prize for which God has called me heavenward in Christ Jesus.

PHILIPPIANS 3:14 NIV

Thank You, Lord, for hearing my prayers and for helping me take action!

AMEN.

WEEK 20

FITNESS

My wife likes to quip, "Young men should do dangerous things so they have stories to tell when they're older."

By the age of thirteen, I was doing "big air," 360-degree, head-over-heels flips on my pre-BMX bicycle. Before I turned eighteen, climbing a sheer ice face on Glacier Peak's Kennedy Ridge, I was hanging one-handed over four hundred feet of vertical air. I still remember waking up one morning and realizing I was married with two kids. . .I needed to stop doing dangerous things.

Thankfully, fitness doesn't require dangerous activity and lots of adrenaline. Surprisingly, the core of fitness comes down to a few basics, including good hydration, a healthy diet, intentional breaks, brisk walking, and hand-picked exercises. Gratefully caring for the body God gave you is actually a form of worship.

Physical training is of some value, but godliness has value for all things, holding promise for both the present life and the life to come.

1 Timothy 4:8 NIV

MONDAY

DRINK LOTS OF WATER

[Jesus said,] "If anyone gives even a cup of cold water to one of these little ones who is my disciple, truly I tell you, that person will certainly not lose their reward."
MATTHEW 10:42 NIV

My friend Wayne mocked the idea of a water backpack for his hike down and back up the Grand Canyon. He had never used one while climbing North America's highest mountains. Staff at the breakfast café tried to convince him, but Wayne wouldn't be dissuaded. *The canyon*, he thought, *is only a mile deep*.

Of course, that vertical mile is made up of many miles of switchbacks that slowly take you to the bottom. When Wayne finished his one plastic bottle of water, he tossed it with plans to retrieve it on the way back. He never did. As the sun filled the canyon and the temperature soared, Wayne passed out. Three women later found him unconscious along the trail.

Without water, we'll last only a few hours in a dry, hot climate or a few days in a cooler, wetter place. Yet many of us compromise our fitness by failing to drink enough. When Jesus promised "living water" (John 4:10), He was describing a spiritual blessing. But isn't it instructive that He used *water* as His example?

Lord, remind me to drink enough water today. It's one of Your greater gifts!

TUESDAY

MAINTAIN A HEALTHY DIET

For everything God created is good, and nothing is to be rejected if it is received with thanksgiving, because it is consecrated by the word of God and prayer.

1 TIMOTHY 4:4–5 NIV

When our two older daughters were fourteen and twelve, they announced they had become vegetarians. I said that was fine, on three conditions: First, *they* had to cook the vegetarian options for dinner. Second, they had to study nutrition for vegetarians. And third, they needed to join me in studying what the Bible says about food.

We quickly discovered that God's Word has a lot to say about what we eat, as far back as Genesis 2. Meat was introduced into the human diet in Genesis 9. In the New Testament we're told to respect both people who eat meat and those who don't. We're also instructed to eat whatever is placed before us (Luke 10:8; 1 Corinthians 10:27). Both of my daughters did exactly that when they later traveled in Africa and China.

One key to healthy eating? Receive whatever you eat *with thanksgiving*.

Lord, I'm grateful for the food You provide.
Please help me to eat wisely and well.

WEDNESDAY

TAKE INTENTIONAL BREAKS

"[Ruth] said, 'Please let me glean and gather among the sheaves behind the harvesters.' She came into the field and has remained here from morning till now, except for a short rest in the shelter."

RUTH 2:7 NIV

One of my favorite childhood experiences was meeting my grandpa as he arrived home from work. Grandma would give us both chocolate chip cookies and milk as grandpa sat in his easy chair. We would tease each other until he invariably fell asleep, getting a quick nap before dinner.

In Bible times, people took intentional breaks as we see in the story of Ruth above. Sometimes the break was an evening nap in a boat (Mark 4:38). Sometimes it was an outdoor nap after eating (1 Kings 19:6). Sometimes it meant sitting in the shade in the heat of the day (Genesis 18:1). Thanks to the examples of Ruth, Jesus, Elijah, and Abraham, we're encouraged to take breaks too—each in our own way.

Sadly, I hated taking breaks during my workday until I was in my late fifties—and my health had greatly diminished. If only I had recognized the necessity of rest much sooner!

Lord, please help me to take intentional breaks from my work. Refresh and renew me.

THURSDAY

ENJOY WALKING

"These words that I command you today shall be on your heart. You shall teach them diligently to your children, and shall talk of them when you sit in your house, and when you walk by the way."
DEUTERONOMY 6:6–7 ESV

I've done a lot of walking, running, and biking. I found each form of exercise refreshing and reinvigorating, and sometimes pretty tiring.

You won't find bikers in the Bible, but the runners include Joseph (when fleeing temptation), David (in combat and fleeing from Saul), and Elijah (racing King Ahab's chariot back to the capital). And don't forget that Jesus told a famous story about a gentleman running to embrace his long-lost prodigal son.

Mostly, however, God's Word talks about walking. During three years of public ministry, Jesus walked through the territory of every tribe of Israel except one. Then again, He had already twice trekked the area of the southernmost tribe, Simeon, with His parents—on the way to and from Egypt as a boy.

I hope you enjoy walking—and do it often. You'll find physical benefits, but also refreshment for your mind and soul.

Lord, help me to add walking to my daily routine. I want to benefit my body, mind, and spirit.

FRIDAY

USE HAND PICKED EXERCISES

Everyone who competes in the games goes into strict training. They do it to get a crown that will not last, but we do it to get a crown that will last forever.
1 CORINTHIANS 9:25 NIV

Throughout history, exercise happened primarily through the vigor of daily living: hauling water, chopping wood, tending gardens, washing clothes, making things, etc. The Greeks had the luxury to put on competitions to demonstrate athletic prowess; but then, like now, few people are Olympians.

Today, we know more than ever about the complex design of the human body—and how to care for it. For some people, exercise is about being as strong and fit as possible. For others, it means using specific exercises to address physical pain or challenges.

My wife's chiropractor always encourages her to start with two simple stretches each morning. Over the past year, she's added several more to her morning routine to address pain in her hip and back. Renée's not winning any medals, but she can walk again without pain.

Find ways to take care of your own body. God's given you just one—so make it last!

Lord, thank You for the incredible design and capability of my body. Guide me in taking the best possible care of it.

DATE: ....

Lord, many guys want an adrenaline rush, but I know that I need to focus on the core of fitness, including moderate physical activity day after day.

5 TOPICS COVERED THIS WEEK:

MONDAY: drink lots of water
TUESDAY: maintain a healthy diet
WEDNESDAY: take intentional breaks
THURSDAY: enjoy walking
FRIDAY: use handpicked exercises

3 WAYS PHYSICAL FITNESS STIMULATES ME:

1 ....

2 ....

3 ....

3 WAYS PHYSICAL FITNESS DISHEARTENS ME:

1 ....

2 ....

3 ....

How I want to respond to these truths:

....

....

....

....

....

....

....

....

LORD, HERE'S WHAT'S GOING ON IN MY LIFE RIGHT NOW. . .

OTHER THINGS I NEED TO SHARE WITH YOU, LORD. . .

Lord, when it comes to this new life map, I need to. . .

Work with your hands, just as we told you, so that your daily life may win the respect of outsiders and so that you will not be dependent on anybody.

1 THESSALONIANS 4:11–12 NIV

Thank You, Lord, for hearing my prayers and for helping me take action!

AMEN.

WEEK 21

TRAVEL

Some people visit all the national parks, and others drive to Grandma's once a year. Some long for tropical paradises; others can't wait to visit historical sites. Some travel out of curiosity, to make connections, or simply to celebrate life.

If you step outside your state, you can experience your great country. If you step outside your country, you can get a bigger taste of this amazing planet. The most important step is to go.

As a young married couple, Renée and I knew a wealthy older widow whose husband had promised to take her all over the world when he retired. But he didn't retire until he was seventy-five; he took her on a single cruise and shortly thereafter passed away. We determined not to make that same mistake.

As a couple, Renée and I have many great memories of trips we've taken around the world. You won't regret the travels *you* plan this week.

> *He makes me lie down in green pastures, he leads me beside quiet waters, he refreshes my soul. He guides me along the right paths for his name's sake.*
>
> Psalm 23:2–3 NIV

MONDAY

WHERE TO GO AND HOW TO GET THERE

I will instruct you and teach you in the way you should go; I will counsel you with my loving eye on you.
Psalm 32:8 NIV

Is there somewhere you've always wanted to go? Dust off that dream today. What would be special about visiting that place? Are there intriguing connections to family, history, literature, or music?

Why not begin planning a trip for the coming year? Revisit your travel dreams periodically, with the goal of actually going.

Remember, travel isn't only a flight or cruise to an exotic location. Road trips offer many joys of their own. And don't be afraid to travel by bus—the ride can be inexpensive, and it's usually quiet. Taking the train might be an even better option. Railroad tracks often provide stunning views.

Now is the time to dream and plan. As Dr. Seuss famously said, "Oh, the places you'll go."

Lord, I thank You for promising to be with me wherever I go. May I experience You in parts of Your world that are new to me.

TUESDAY

TRAVEL TIPS

"The Lord himself goes before you and will be with you; he will never leave you nor forsake you. Do not be afraid."
Deuteronomy 31:8 niv

Wherever you go, find something to appreciate, even if it's less than you expected. Our tiny hotel room in Paris didn't provide the best night's sleep, but we were there to have new experiences—not replicate home.

Our friend Drenda travels the world, but her most treasured memory is celebrating her husband Don's birthday in Rome. They sat outside on a restaurant patio, drank espresso, and watched people for two hours in front of the Pantheon. You don't experience thousands of years of history like that back home, so take advantage of every moment.

Sign up for tours, but not all of them. City tours offer insights and take you places you might not find on your own. But it's also good to leave plenty of time just to wander.

And be sure to enjoy the cuisine. You haven't experienced a culture until you've tasted the food. Use discretion (don't drink the water!), but do try out local dishes. Oh, and pack the Pepto Bismol.

Wherever you go, remember that God is with you—cheering you on!

Lord, I'd like to know more of the world You have created. Guide me into the places You want me to see.

WEDNESDAY

TRAVEL MISTAKES

The Lord makes firm the steps of the one who delights in him.
Psalm 37:23 NIV

Tips to minimize travel mistakes:

(1) Don't dress to impress when you travel. Traveling light costs less—and leaves room for souvenirs. (2) Allow time for spontaneous adventures. After all, you might meet someone who invites you to a local event. Join in the fun! (3) Don't try to visit too many destinations. You can't see a tenth of all the museums in Washington, DC, in four days. And don't try to see Rome, Paris, Florence, or Venice in a week. (4) Remember: "Everyone vacations in their own way." Talk ahead of time about what you're most looking forward to doing. Do you love having a leisurely breakfast and then reading for an hour, or do you prefer getting up and exploring right away? Make sure you travel with family or friends who have the physical health, stamina, and ability to enjoy the activities you want to do. Take into account preferences for sleeping and eating schedules—and just how flexible each person is. Allow for time for people to do their own thing.

The biggest travel mistake? Not going!

Lord, please give me wisdom and flexibility to travel well—to get the most from my experience.

THURSDAY

PLAN AND PAY FOR TRAVEL

If I rise on the wings of the dawn, if I settle on the far side of the sea, even there your hand will guide me, your right hand will hold me fast.

Psalm 139:9–10 NIV

If you plan ahead, you can travel more often than you might guess. Why not start a travel savings account? If you use direct deposit from your paycheck, designate perhaps thirty dollars for this account. After a few months, consider increasing that amount.

Learn to use online booking sites and find the ones that work best for you. Consider booking flights to secondary airports—sometimes flights are much less expensive if you're willing to travel, say, a hundred miles by car.

When using small airlines, watch for hidden costs, and allow for the greater possibility of delayed and cancelled flights. Using these airlines for solo or unhurried travel makes more sense than when you're traveling with children or on a tight schedule.

Of course, you can always take a road trip, packing your own food to save money. Visit or swap houses with friends in different areas of the country. There are plenty of travel options—the important thing is to get out and see God's world!

Lord, please help me to budget carefully and set aside money for future travel. I want a bigger perspective on the world You've given us.

FRIDAY

MAKE TRAVEL MEANINGFUL

The Lord will watch over your coming and going both now and forevermore.
Psalm 121:8 NIV

Travel takes you away from your everyday responsibilities and transports you somewhere new. Whether your trip is exciting, educational, or restful, it promises more than just a good time. Travel expands your perspectives about other people.

Make travel more meaningful by studying the places you plan to visit. Read their history, but also check out their current challenges. Consider how you can support the economy during your visit. Meet some local residents. I took our younger son on a road trip down the Oregon coast. Ben loved visiting small towns off the beaten path so he could ask shop owners for their stories.

Travel to serve. Helping to build a small home in an impoverished town blesses you just as much as the receiving family. Visiting missionaries and seeing their world means so much to them. Give the gift of listening and helping with physical tasks or ministry. And still see the sights!

Best of all, return home with a bigger sense of God's heart for the world.

Lord, I thank You that I can be blessed and a blessing when I travel.

Lord, I want to dream, plan, schedule, travel, and return home with a greater appreciation for this world and a bigger sense of Your heart for people.

5 TOPICS COVERED THIS WEEK:

MONDAY: where to go and how to get there
TUESDAY: travel tips
WEDNESDAY: travel mistakes
THURSDAY: plan and pay for travel
FRIDAY: make travel meaningful

3 WAYS TRAVEL APPEALS TO ME:

1 ....

2 ....

3 ....

3 WAYS TRAVEL CONCERNS ME:

1 ....

2 ....

3 ....

How I want to respond to these truths:

....

....

....

....

....

....

....

....

LORD, HERE'S WHAT'S GOING ON IN MY LIFE RIGHT NOW. . .

OTHER THINGS I NEED TO SHARE WITH YOU, LORD. . .

Lord, when it comes to this new life map, I need to. . .

We plan the way we want to live, but only God makes us able to live it.

Proverbs 16:9 MSG

Thank You, Lord, for hearing my prayers and for helping me take action!

AMEN.

WEEK 22

FINANCES, PART 1

When it comes to finances, the apostle Paul is my hero. He could say, "I have learned to be content whatever the circumstances" (Philippians 4:11 NIV). Don't miss that word *learned*.

As a younger man, a member of the Pharisees, Paul (then known as Saul) was probably wealthy—likely a man who loved money (see Luke 16:14). As an apostle, however, he repeatedly lost his possessions to theft, riots, imprisonment, and shipwreck. As a result, he had known thirst and hunger, often going without food. Paul had even been cold and naked at times (see 2 Corinthians 11:23–27). He consistently worked hard to provide for his own needs and the needs of others (see Acts 18:3, Ephesians 4:28, 1 Thessalonians 4:11–12, 2 Thessalonians 3:6–15). Philippians 4:11 is not theory. Paul lived it out for decades—and we can too.

It's clear that Paul wasn't against wealth. He said in Philippians 4:12 (NIV), "I know what it is to be in need, and I know what it is to have plenty. I have learned the secret of being content in any and every situation, whether well fed or hungry, whether living in plenty or in want."

If I could give one gift to every Christian, it would be this conviction: that "godliness with contentment is great gain" (1 Timothy 6:6 NIV).

Wealth gained hastily will dwindle, but whoever gathers little by little will increase it.

PROVERBS 13:11 ESV

MONDAY

MONTHLY NET INCOME

Make it your goal to live a quiet life,
minding your own business and working.
1 THESSALONIANS 4:11 NLT

Paul is certainly right: "godliness with contentment is great gain." Toward that end, we're going to discuss income and expenses during this first of two weeks on Finances.

Today, we focus on income. *Gross* income is what you earn before deductions. *Net* income is what you take home after taxes, benefit cost-sharing, and miscellaneous fees.

Do you know your current gross and net? If not, look up your latest pay stub or flip back to last year's W-2. It's important to know exactly what your monthly net income is, as well as your monthly expenses.

When your net income is greater than expenses, month after month and year after year, good things are happening for you and your family. It means no cash flow problems, extra money always on hand for emergencies, and growing prosperity. You'll have healthy savings and a growing retirement account.

Bottom line: Seek contentment now by consistently spending *less* than your net income; your wealth will build over time.

Lord, I thank You for the ability to earn income and spend wisely. Help me to carefully mind what You've given me.

TUESDAY

INCOME STREAMS

Remember the Lord your God, for it is he who gives you the ability to produce wealth.

DEUTERONOMY 8:18 NIV

In today's on-demand world, anyone who with an extra room, car, time, skills, or stuff can pursue income streams via any number of online services. It just takes a few smarts.

Of course, anyone can *lose* money as fast as they make it. I have a friend, Steve, who drives people for a ride service. One of his customers was excited about selling a purse to someone across town for a hundred dollars. When the ride was over, though, the customer's tab was $99.76. So much for smarts. . .

Later, Steve himself started wondering if driving for a ride service was a real job or just a hobby. After calculating his costs for gas and wear-and-tear on his Toyota Camry, Steve discovered he was netting about four dollars an hour. So he quickly began searching for a real job. Scoring the latter wasn't fun, but it did wonders for Steve's monthly income.

When you need more income, seek it out—but beware of increasing your hours or stress. If a promotion or new job takes a while to gain, that's okay. Better to wait than to make a costly mistake.

Lord, You give me the ability to produce wealth. Please help me to use that ability wisely.

WEDNESDAY

FIRST EXPENSES

Remember the words of the Lord Jesus:
"It is more blessed to give than to receive."
Acts 20:35 NLT

When you create a budget, at the top is space for Income. Below that, you'll capture Expenses.

The first expense category is involuntary—it includes federal, state, regional, and local taxes and fees.

The second expense category may or may not be voluntary. For example, employer-employee benefit cost-sharing includes health insurance and retirement contributions. If your employer matches the latter by a strong percentage, make sure you add a voluntary contribution of your own.

The third expense is completely voluntary, and it reflects your faith and trust in God and His Word. Such expenses include tithe and offerings to your local church and its missionaries.

As the Lord leads, we love to do extra giving, like paying for a new water heater for a family down the street. Renée and I also keep a hundred-dollar bill in our wallets "just in case." We believe, as Jesus said, giving is more blessed than receiving!

Lord, thank You for the reminder to give.
Increase my sensitivity and generosity.

THURSDAY

MONTHLY EXPENSES

"Won't you first sit down and estimate the cost to see if you have enough money?"
LUKE 14:28 NIV

On your personal budget sheet, directly under EXPENSES are two categories: BEFORE NET and AFTER NET.

BEFORE NET includes taxes, fees, benefit cost-sharing, and anything else deducted from your take-home pay. AFTER NET includes two more categories: MONTHLY and DAILY.

Monthly expenses to factor in to your budget include insurance policy costs and your rent or mortgage. The latter should include a prorated amount for the upkeep of your home and yard. (Words of wisdom: Don't take on debt to remodel your kitchen or install a new roof. Instead, over time, set aside money each month toward such future expenses.)

Your budget should also list your monthly car payments, student loans, and any other expenses, as well as charges you've incurred on your credit card and bank account.

And then there are the utility payments: oil, propane, natural gas, electricity, water, garbage, recycling, Internet, phone, and the like. Prorate any that are billed bimonthly or quarterly.

The more you can reduce your monthly expenses, the more you'll have to put toward more important things. Christians have plenty of those.

Lord, I'm glad You know every part of my budget in detail. Help me to do the same!

FRIDAY

DAILY EXPENSES

"I have not coveted anyone's silver or gold or clothing. You yourselves know that these hands of mine have supplied my own needs and the needs of my companions."

Acts 20:33–34 niv

In the verse above, Paul isn't speaking against silver or gold, and he certainly has no complaint with clothing. But we all know that money and things can be very attractive to our human nature.

We enjoy *seeing* nice things. As we prosper, we might also enjoy *owning* such things. The apostle's secret was to be content both when he possessed things, and when they were lost due to wear and tear, accident, theft, imprisonment. . .or worse.

For many of us, accumulating nice, quality things happens after we've learned to control our daily expenses. One key in doing that is to track every expenditure you make. If you're married, you want your wife on the same page (figuratively), tracking everything she spends on her own page (literally). These pages should be readily available to everyone in the family so your children can learn how to budget as well.

Next week, we'll discuss non-budgetary matters that will help you prosper financially. But before that, don't miss this weekend's life map on the next two pages!

Lord, You know all of my wants and needs.
Help me to know the difference between them.

Lord, I want to own this conviction: "Godliness with contentment is great gain" (1 Timothy 6:6 NIV*). What a difference that conviction could make in my life now—and for years to come!*

5 TOPICS COVERED THIS WEEK:

MONDAY: monthly net income
TUESDAY: income streams
WEDNESDAY: first expenses
THURSDAY: monthly expenses
FRIDAY: daily expenses

3 WAYS A BUDGET CAN HELP ME:

1 ....
2 ....
3 ....

3 WAYS A BUDGET CAN FRUSTRATE ME:

1 ....
2 ....
3 ....

How I want to respond to these truths:

....
....
....
....
....
....
....
....

LORD, HERE'S WHAT'S GOING ON IN MY LIFE RIGHT NOW. . .

OTHER THINGS I NEED TO SHARE WITH YOU, LORD. . .

Lord, when it comes to this new life map, I need to. . .

Keep your lives free from the love of money and be content with what you have, because God has said, "Never will I leave you; never will I forsake you."

HEBREWS 13:5 NIV

Thank You, Lord, for hearing my prayers and for helping me take action!

AMEN.

WEEK 23

FINANCES, PART 2

Experience is the best teacher—*especially other people's experiences.* This is doubly true when it comes to finances. Skip other weeks in this book, but not this one! God wants you to "act smart" by applying knowledge, discernment, understanding, and wisdom to your finances. Your life is too short to waste money.

A dozen individuals and couples used this week's financial advice for a year and reported saving tens of thousands of dollars. You're sure to come out way ahead too!

We'll discuss smart ways to find a financial adviser, to purchase insurance, to avoid high-rate debt, to correct financial mistakes, and to deal with catastrophic medical crises.

By week's end, you'll have the knowledge to reap substantial financial rewards for a lifetime.

The blessing of the Lord makes rich,
and he adds no sorrow with it.
Proverbs 10:22 ESV

MONDAY

FIND A FINANCIAL ADVISER

Wisdom is found in those who take advice.
PROVERBS 13:10 NIV

Throughout this book, I've been offering insights into many life topics, including your finances, and I'll continue to do so. But your specific situation will always be best served by a financial adviser who knows you personally.

When I say "financial adviser," I don't necessarily mean a licensed professional. If you have some resources and the wherewithal to pay for a respected and recommended professional, then certainly do so. But until you reach that point, you may find some great, free advice from your dad, an older businessman at church, or some other successful individual you know. They can provide wise insights on issues such as buying versus renting a home, how and when and where to purchase a car, and what kinds of investments may be tailor-made for your situation.

We often think we can "go it alone," but the life experience of older men we know and trust can be a huge advantage to our own futures. Plus, they'll probably enjoy sharing their insights!

Lord, may I always be a man who takes advice—especially in this important area of finances.

TUESDAY

BUY ESSENTIAL INSURANCE COVERAGE

For the protection of wisdom is like the protection of money, and the advantage of knowledge is that wisdom preserves the life of him who has it.

Ecclesiastes 7:12 ESV

Not all insurance policies are created equal. You want to choose the companies and policies that best fit *your* needs. Thankfully, you probably need to buy only five policies.

First, health insurance. Co-pays don't matter quite as much as deductibles do. Know what you're getting and how much it will cost you.

Second, disability insurance. No one plans to turn fifty or sixty and suddenly become disabled, but that can happen. Decades ago, my friend Gordon and I both bought disability insurance policies—and ended up needing them. Gordon's policy is great. Mine only paid five hundred dollars a month. Ouch!

Third, term life insurance. Look for a low monthly price that's locked in for the next twenty or thirty years. After a few years, if you're building a family, it's wise to buy a second policy.

Fourth, auto insurance. Buy comprehensive, not collision.

Fifth, homeowners insurance. Make sure "flood" is covered in case, for example, a dishwasher hose springs a leak. Water, like fire, creates a lot of costly damage in a hurry.

Lord, may I always trust You—but also prepare prudently for the future. Give me wisdom as I consider insurance.

WEDNESDAY

FLEE HIGH-RATE LOANS

The rich rule over the poor, and the borrower is slave to the lender.
PROVERBS 22:7 NIV

Loan costs can vary dramatically. So you need to have a plan to either avoid or diligently pay off any high-rate loans.

Even if the interest rate starts at 0 percent, *never* use cash advances from credit cards to boost the size of your proposed house down payment. There's no way you'll be able to pay off that much money before you're hammered with 23 percent to 30 percent interest. Suddenly, you no longer owe $12,000. Instead, you owe $18,000. . .and then $23,000. . .and are hopelessly upside down financially.

Don't let that happen! Except for your wife and kids, everything in your house needs a price tag. Sell as much as you can to apply the money to your worst loan. Then sell *more* stuff to pay off any other high-rate loan. If necessary, take a second job for a while to knock out this kind of debt.

One final word: never co-sign someone else's loan. Nearly 90 percent of the time you'll end up paying a terrible loan for *their* car, or boat, or whatever. Just a word to the wise.

Lord, You have warned me against becoming a slave to high-rate loans. Help me to handle my money wisely, save patiently, and avoid wasteful situations.

THURSDAY

CORRECT SMALL FINANCIAL MISTAKES

Then [Jesus] said to them, "Watch out! Be on your guard against all kinds of greed; life does not consist in an abundance of possessions."
LUKE 12:15 NIV

When you make a small financial mistake, don't ignore it. Instead, take immediate action to un-make it.

If you've just bought something you realize you can't afford, return it or exchange it for something you can. If you've incurred a first-time overdraft charge, drop by your bank, apologize, promise it will never happen again, and ask, "This one time, is there any way this overdraft charge could be reversed?" The phrase "This one time" is crucial. So is the phrase "Is there any way. . . ?" If the answer is no, don't say anything. Just silently count to ten. The teller may study your eyes, go talk with the manager, and say yes, "This one time." If you've incurred a first-time late payment fee, follow the same guidance online or over the phone.

It never hurts to ask.

Lord, give me wisdom in making my financial decisions. . .but if I do the wrong thing, prompt me to un-make that mistake immediately.

FRIDAY

RESPONDING TO HUGE HOSPITAL DEBTS

God is able to bless you abundantly, so that in all things at all times, having all that you need, you will abound in every good work.
2 CORINTHIANS 9:8 NIV

If you're ever hit with catastrophic medical bills, don't immediately think bankruptcy. Come back to this book and reread this page. And feel free to share this information with any family members or friends who find themselves in this situation.

As I write this, America has slightly more than twenty-nine hundred community hospitals. The IRS recognizes 59 percent of them as non-profit. This includes the majority of hospitals with religious terms in their names, words such as Adventist, Beth, Holy, Providence, Sacred, Saint, Samaritan, Sinai, and Sister.

These hospitals often have a benevolence fund that is sometimes overseen by a related charitable foundation. Each is required to give away a certain amount of money every year. Sometimes those funds are put into medical research, buildings, equipment, and staff. Other funds are used to help people who find it difficult, if not impossible, to pay their hospital bills.

What a relief—and what a great reminder of the way God forgives us.

Lord, I'm grateful that You are a forgiving God—and that You encourage others to follow Your example.

DATE:

Lord, life is too short to waste money. Help me to "act smart" by applying knowledge, discernment, understanding, and wisdom to my finances.

5 TOPICS COVERED THIS WEEK:

MONDAY: find a financial adviser
TUESDAY: buy essential insurance coverage
WEDNESDAY: flee high-rate loans
THURSDAY: correct small financial mistakes
FRIDAY: responding to huge hospital debts

3 WAYS MONEY MANAGEMENT EXCITES ME:

1 ....

2 ....

3 ....

3 WAYS MONEY MANAGEMENT FRUSTRATES ME:

1 ....

2 ....

3 ....

How I want to respond to these truths:

LORD, HERE'S WHAT'S GOING ON IN MY LIFE RIGHT NOW. . .

OTHER THINGS I NEED TO SHARE WITH YOU, LORD. . .

Lord, when it comes to this new life map, I need to. . .

"For where your treasure is, there your heart will be also."

MATTHEW 6:21 NIV

Thank You, Lord, for hearing my prayers and for helping me take action!

AMEN.

WEEK 24

GIVING BACK, PART 1

Jesus rarely made statements that are easy to believe. Take His words, "You're far happier giving than getting" (Acts 20:35 MSG). Too good to be true? Well, actually, lots of scientifically backed research has documented this counterintuitive reality.

"Giving back" includes volunteer service, community leadership, financial contributions, and relational support. Among the many benefits that you'll enjoy are personal happiness, lowered stress, and an improved immune system. Givers report greater satisfaction with life, more meaning in life, more friends, and stronger relationships. They know they've helped to make others happier.

Want some more benefits to giving back? How about a more positive outlook on life, improved mental health, deeper contentment, higher self-esteem, and improved spiritual vitality. And don't forget the *eternal* rewards.

Never be lacking in zeal, but keep your spiritual fervor, serving the Lord.

ROMANS 12:11 NIV

MONDAY

SERVE AT YOUR CHURCH

Always give yourselves fully to the work of the Lord,
because you know that your labor in the Lord is not in vain.
1 CORINTHIANS 15:58 NIV

When I started attending my current church many years ago, I fell in love with the people and quickly volunteered to serve. "We don't do it that way," I was told. "Just sit back and be part of the church family for six months. Then let's see where you might serve."

I ended up going to a second church to work with their youth group during that time. Looking back, I realize I was being foolish. I should have given much more priority to "be part of the church family." Thankfully, I've made up for my impulsiveness every year since.

If your church has policies about who can serve, when and where, be grateful—and do whatever you can to fulfill each requirement. Then ask which volunteer opportunities are open, check out one or two ministries to find your best fit, and offer your services.

God gifts every vibrant church with enough volunteers. Always make sure you are doing your part.

Lord, I want to serve in church as a sign of my gratitude to You. Guide me into the best role, I pray.

TUESDAY

LIVE LIKE AN ELDER

The elders who direct the affairs of the church well are worthy of double honor, especially those whose work is preaching and teaching.

1 Timothy 5:17 NIV

God wants every man of faith to live like an elder. We see this in 1 Timothy 3:1–7, Titus 1:5–9, and 1 Peter 5:1–4. In these three passages, we're told that elders care for, shepherd, pastor, lead, and oversee the local church. While some elders are recognized with official titles, most aren't. They're the guys who *live* like elders, regardless of age, education, or public recognition.

Living like elders, men of faith learn to teach the truths of the Word of God—whether formally or informally. They protect the church from false teachers. They prayerfully and carefully evaluate questions of faith and practice.

Just as importantly, elders pray for their fellow brothers and sisters, anoint those who are sick, and visit the imprisoned. They embody the good news of Jesus Christ in every sphere of life and maintain a good reputation in the community.

Again, this isn't for a select few. This is for *every* Christian man—including you.

Lord, You have expectations for every Christian man. May I live up to the potential You've given me.

WEDNESDAY

GIVE TO YOUR CHURCH

Each of you should give what you have decided in your heart to give, not reluctantly or under compulsion, for God loves a cheerful giver.
2 CORINTHIANS 9:7 NIV

If you grew up in a churchgoing family, you may remember taking coins from your allowance to put in the offering plate. If you've only recently started attending church, maybe you're not so sure what the offering is all about. That's okay—even many long-time, committed Christians haven't budgeted for regular giving to their church.

Television preachers are often too pushy about money, so many local pastors hesitate to teach on giving. They don't want to enhance a negative stereotype. But God does call Christians to support their local church—and not just when they feel like it or for special projects, but in a consistent, dependable way.

Our church gets by on a tight budget. I might not think my own giving contributes that much, but joined with the regular gifts of others, the church is enabled to minister to its people and our community. What really matters is your decision to give regularly and cheerfully to God's work.

Lord, please give me a heart willing to give from what You've given me.

THURSDAY

DONATE TO THE BENEVOLENCE FUND

"In everything I did, I showed you that by this kind of hard work we must help the weak, remembering the words the Lord Jesus himself said: 'It is more blessed to give than to receive.'"

ACTS 20:35 NIV

One rainy morning Renée stopped our old car at an intersection only two blocks from our house. A sports car racing down the hill lost control, hit our vehicle, and tore off most of the front end. Thankfully, Renée was completely unharmed—but the insurance settlement was far short of what we needed to buy another used car. Almost immediately, a woman at church loaned us her extra car. Two Sundays later, Renée and I received a twenty-five-hundred-dollar benevolence gift. We were completely surprised, but what an answer to prayer!

Our church has two benevolence funds: The first is for church members, the second for outside requests from the community. Both funds distribute thousands of dollars annually. Believe me, someone always is in need.

Churches generally don't talk a lot about their benevolence funds, But they can be vital to many people. Why not ask your pastor if your church has one—and if it needs more donations to keep it strong.

Lord, please help me to meet needs—whether individually or through my church's benevolent fund. May my generosity point people to Jesus!

FRIDAY

SUPPORT ONE OF YOUR MISSIONARIES

These women were helping to support [Jesus and the Twelve] out of their own means.

LUKE 8:3 NIV

Not every church sends out missionaries from its own congregation. Our medium-sized church, however, has been something of an overachiever in that regard. Well over a dozen of our close friends have been sent as missionaries to Africa, Asia, Europe, and Latin America. Renée and I contribute to their support through our local church, and then we help roll out the red carpet when they come home on furloughs.

Many churches contribute to the support of missionaries sent out by other churches. Those missionaries may visit only once every few years, but modern technology makes it easy to keep in touch via email, social media, phone calls, and video conferencing.

As God leads you, sign up to receive the newsletters from your favorite missionaries. Be sure to connect with them via email and social media. As you get to know each other better, contribute funds via your church for their support. Such financial gifts are "acceptable and pleasing to God" (Philippians 4:18 NLT).

Lord, please show me a missionary to support, both with money and with prayers and correspondence. Use my gifts to make a difference around the world.

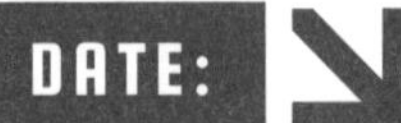

Lord, I thank You for the many benefits of "giving back": greater happiness, lower stress, greater satisfaction, more friends, and eternal rewards.

5 TOPICS COVERED THIS WEEK:

MONDAY: serve at your church
TUESDAY: live like an elder
WEDNESDAY: give to your church
THURSDAY: donate to the benevolence fund
FRIDAY: support one of your missionaries

3 WAYS GIVING BACK APPEALS TO ME:

1 ....
2 ....
3 ....

3 WAYS GIVING BACK CONCERNS ME:

1 ....
2 ....
3 ....

How I want to respond to these truths:

....
....
....
....
....
....
....
....

LORD, HERE'S WHAT'S GOING ON IN MY LIFE RIGHT NOW. . .

OTHER THINGS I NEED TO SHARE WITH YOU, LORD. . .

Lord, when it comes to this new life map, I need to. . .

And this same God who takes care of me will supply all your needs from his glorious riches, which have been given to us in Christ Jesus.

PHILIPPIANS 4:19 NLT

Thank You, Lord, for hearing my prayers and for helping me take action!

AMEN.

WEEK 25

GIVING BACK, PART 2

This past week we highlighted the many benefits of generosity, whether you are serving at your church, living like an elder, or contributing to your church offering, benevolence fund, and missionaries.

This week, we'll explore five even more active ideas for giving back: visiting a missionary overseas, hosting a refugee family, sponsoring a needy child, serving as a foster parent, and considering adoption.

In each of these areas, you may have to stretch way outside your comfort zone and depend on the Lord more than any other time in your life. These are challenging tasks! But the experiences will add amazing highlights in your life map.

Renée and I have never had "enough money" to do these things—but we always felt the Lord prompting us to step out in faith. I hope that's your experience five times over.

> *"Test me in this," says the Lord Almighty, "and see if I will not throw open the floodgates of heaven and pour out so much blessing that there will not be room enough to store it."*
>
> Malachi 3:10 NIV

MONDAY

VISIT A MISSIONARY OVERSEAS

Leaving the next day, we reached Caesarea and stayed at the house of Philip the evangelist, one of the Seven.
ACTS 21:8 NIV

During a Christmas party, Renée and I talked with some good friends, Greg and Gwen. They gave us updates on a big trip they were planning to visit three of our church's missionaries on the Pacific coast of Peru. "We're so jealous," Renée said. "I'd love to take a trip like that someday," I added. Greg and Gwen looked at each other, then back at us. It turned out Gwen had just learned she was pregnant. So Greg asked with a smile, "Would you be willing to go in our place?"

How could we say no? But what in the world had we just signed up for?

More recent trips to visit our church's missionaries have been much more intentional on our part. Sometimes Renée or I travel solo, but usually we go together. All told, we've spent two weeks in Africa, two months in South America, and a month in Europe. On each occasion, we've sought to see our missionary friends doing life. Any ministry that they or we do is extra, not essential. That may sound backwards, but it's exactly what the missionaries need.

Why not start praying about which of your church's missionaries you might visit?

Lord, put a missionary on my heart, and show me if and how I should plan a visit.

TUESDAY

HOST A REFUGEE COUPLE

There was an estate nearby that belonged to Publius, the chief official of the island. He welcomed us to his home and showed us generous hospitality.
ACTS 28:7 NIV

After the fall of Saigon, Vietnam, in 1975, Renée's parents hosted not one, not two, but *three* refugee couples who had escaped communism and come to the United States. They knew little or no English, and they had no idea how life worked here in America—but they wanted to learn, and fast. In time, each family became successful in its own right. What a joy to see their children thrive and start families of their own. Six soon will be fifty! They've brought such joy to my family through the years.

Some refugee couples and families live for a while with sponsors, but most now receive their own government-subsidized apartments. Most of them have enough money to purchase what they need to live on. What they really need are American families who welcome them, help them practice English, and answer their questions. Our family's motto: There are no dumb questions—especially if your guests ask why you're being so helpful. What an opportunity to share the gospel!

Lord, open my heart to needy people from around the world, and show me how I might become a help to them.

WEDNESDAY

SPONSOR A NEEDY CHILD

Defend the weak and the fatherless;
uphold the cause of the poor and the oppressed.
PSALM 82:3 NIV

Years ago, my good friends Luis and Pat Palau, who traveled the world for decades, visited child sponsorship programs in many countries. Their conclusion: the best program is Compassion International, based in Colorado Springs, Colorado. Many years later, our family still sponsors and prays regularly for specific children through the organization.

It's easy to sign up to sponsor a needy child. Just be sure you're ready to make a long-term commitment. There's nothing worse than for a child to learn that David Sanford is his sponsor, then being told that Mr. Sanford has decided to *stop* sponsoring him. Sponsorships are one part of our budget that we will not cut.

Today, sponsorship is easier and more interactive than ever. Renée and I automatically have monthly payments deducted from our checking account. And we use the organization's website to correspond with each child, send and receive photos and artwork, and make special contributions to their family for birthdays and Christmas.

Knowing how Jesus loved children, it just seems right.

Lord, please bless the needy children of the world—
and let me know how I might play a part in that.

THURSDAY

SERVE AS A FOSTER PARENT

Learn to do right; seek justice. Defend the oppressed. Take up the cause of the fatherless.

ISAIAH 1:17 NIV

Renée and I had just signed up for foster-parent training when she received a call from a caseworker. Could we take two neglected girls, ages five and eight, *right now*? I was on a business trip, so Renée called me. We agreed. Nine months later, our foster girls were reunited with their birth mom. Today those girls are married with families of their own.

Every day in America hundreds of thousands of children are in foster care. They didn't ask to be placed there. Instead, their parents or guardians somehow neglected or abused them. These kids need a place to call home until they can either be reunified with their parent or placed in an adoptive family.

It isn't easy to care for a troubled child or deal with the social service system. You give your heart with no guarantees—but isn't that like Jesus' love?

If you simply can't open your home to a foster child, find a foster family and offer to help. Be their biggest fan and advocate. Together you can give a child a future and hope.

Lord, fostering a child is a huge commitment—but please show me how I might become involved.

FRIDAY

CONSIDER ADOPTION

Religion that God our Father accepts as pure and faultless is this: to look after orphans and widows in their distress and to keep oneself from being polluted by the world.
James 1:27 NIV

Renée and I had always considered growing our family through adoption. After our two foster girls were reunited with their birth mom, we prayerfully and carefully reevaluated our adoption plans. Did we still want to adopt? Yes, absolutely. Were we ready to pursue adoption at that point? No—we waited until our biological children were a bit older before adopting our youngest daughter.

Adoption is part of our family's experience. Our daughter and son-in-law adopted Nathan at birth and have a strong relationship with his birth mother. Other family members have adopted children from orphanages overseas or within the extended family.

When you adopt, you're committing your whole life to a particular child no matter what. When adoptive children have experienced trauma, raising them probably won't look the same as raising birth children. Adoptive parents need every resource and helper they can get.

In the United States, the average age of children needing an adoptive home is *six*. Might God be nudging you to consider giving one of them a home?

Lord, this is a huge question, but You are far bigger. Guide me in Your perfect way, for Your own glory.

DATE:

Lord, stretch me outside my comfort zone so that I depend on You more than ever. Show me the hard things You want me to do—things that will add amazing highlights in my life.

5 TOPICS COVERED THIS WEEK:

MONDAY: visit a missionary overseas
TUESDAY: host a refugee couple
WEDNESDAY: sponsor a needy child
THURSDAY: serve as a foster parent
FRIDAY: consider adoption

3 WAYS GIVING SACRIFICIALLY BLESSES ME:

1.

2.

3.

3 WAYS GIVING SACRIFICIALLY WORRIES ME:

1.

2.

3.

How I want to respond to these truths:

LORD, HERE'S WHAT'S GOING ON IN MY LIFE RIGHT NOW. . .

OTHER THINGS I NEED TO SHARE WITH YOU, LORD. . .

Lord, when it comes to this new life map, I need to. . .

But he [God Almighty] knows the way that I take; when he has tested me, I will come forth as gold.

JOB 23:10 NIV

Thank You, Lord, for hearing my prayers and for helping me take action!

AMEN.

WEEK 26

FINISHING WELL, PART 1

Billy Graham. What a life! What a legacy! Yet Billy Graham made it clear in the early 1980s that his ministry could be over in a moment. "If I should ever take any glory away from God," he said, "God would take His hand off my life and my lips would turn to clay." It's a sobering thought that the Lord could nullify what any given individual does best.

Renowned research professor J. Robert Clinton has invested much of his career analyzing why people do—or don't—finish well. He once did a comparative study of the lives of more than eight hundred Christian leaders, concluding that "few leaders finish well."

Clinton lists six barriers to finishing well, including unresolved sin. This week, we'll look at the other five barriers: (1) the misuse of money; (2) the abuse of power; (3) unchecked pride; (4) illicit sexual relationships; and (5) unresolved family problems.

We'll consider biblical truths to keep us safe and productive throughout life.

Let us not become weary in doing good, for at the proper time we will reap a harvest if we do not give up.

Galatians 6:9 niv

MONDAY

THE MISUSE OF MONEY

He [Judas Iscariot] was a thief; as keeper of the money bag, he used to help himself to what was put into it.

JOHN 12:6 NIV

From the first time he "borrowed" a little money from the apostles' fund to the moment he pocketed thirty pieces of silver (Matthew 26:14–16), Judas was looking out for his own interests.

When he objected to a woman's lavish pouring of perfume on Jesus, it wasn't because Judas cared about the poor. What Jesus saw as an act of worship, Judas calculated as a loss of funds to pilfer (John 12:1–6). With ease, Satan entered Judas' heart, propelling him to cut a deal with the leading priests to betray Jesus (Luke 22:1–6).

Even when Judas was later filled with remorse, he never turned back to God in repentance. He simply regretted the tragic turn of events and took what appeared to be the easiest way out: suicide (Matthew 27:5).

Scripture warns strongly against the idea of following the Lord as a means to financial gain (1 Peter 1:13–19; 2 Peter 2:1–16). However Judas began with Jesus, he ended very poorly. Let's value our Lord far above wealth—for who He is, not for what He might give us.

Lord, I want to value You far above all other things. Warn me in those moments when I stray.

TUESDAY

THE ABUSE OF POWER

Then Absalom sent secret messengers throughout the tribes of Israel to say, "As soon as you hear the sound of the trumpets, then say, 'Absalom is king in Hebron.' "
2 Samuel 15:10 niv

In many ways, Absalom was the perfect politician. Then again, Absalom pursued what he wanted in all the wrong ways—for all the wrong reasons. He kept going his way, not God's, to right the supposed wrongs in his life and to gain the power he thought he deserved.

In his desire to be king, Absalom looked not to God's will, but to his own. He decided that he alone should call all the shots—and plotted to take the kingdom of Israel by cunning and force. Even if that meant destroying his father, King David.

Absalom had what it took to be a national leader—political sense, excellent counsel, leadership skills, and even good looks. Yet he grabbed at personal power rather than seeking God's best. And the hand that grabbed for more and more came up empty.

It is only when our hands are open before God, seeking His glory, that He can fill them with blessing and power.

Lord, I want to seek Your will far above my own.
Stop me if I ever try to abuse earthly power.

WEDNESDAY

UNCHECKED PRIDE

Asa was angry with the seer because of this;
he was so enraged that he put him in prison. At the same
time Asa brutally oppressed some of the people.
2 Chronicles 16:10 NIV

Asa was a "white sheep" of the family—the godly son of wicked parents. From the beginning of his kingship, he determined to reign differently than his father, Abijah. Asa set his course to seek the Lord, and God overwhelmingly blessed him for it.

Unfortunately, when Asa was old, his will became his own. Asa looked to human resources to rescue him from enemies, and then bristled when confronted. In pride, he kept looking to human help alone, even for his physical well-being. He died without calling to the Lord even once. How tragic!

If Asa had died only a few years earlier, he would have been known as one of Judah's greatest kings. Instead, he finished abysmally.

Asa's failed life should prompt each of us to ask, "When I am old, will I still look for God's divine help at every step? Or will I have developed my own way of handling life?"

Lord, I want to repent of unchecked pride in my life.
I acknowledge You as the King of my life, now and forever.

THURSDAY

ILLICIT SEXUAL RELATIONSHIPS

One day Samson went to Gaza, where he saw a prostitute. He went in to spend the night with her.
JUDGES 16:1 NIV

The account of Samson covers more chapters in the book of Judges than any other character. The stories tell of Samson's supernaturally foretold birth, the Lord's blessing on his childhood, his lifelong Nazirite vow, the Spirit's hold on his life, his incredible strength. . .and his unbridled passions and lusts.

Samson's story is tragically short. One can only imagine how much more he could have done for the Lord. If Samson hadn't been ruined by his passions and lusts, perhaps an entire book of the Bible would have been written about him.

Like Samson, you and I have a life story to write. And like Samson, we have important choices to make. Samson mistakenly thought he was strong enough to bear the growing weight of his sexual sins. It's a burden that crushed the strongest man in the world—Satan would love to see it crush us too.

Lord, I don't want to be ruled by passions and lusts. Help me to acknowledge You as sovereign over every area of my life.

FRIDAY

UNRESOLVED FAMILY PROBLEMS

[Eli said,] "No, my sons; the report I hear spreading among the LORD's people is not good."
1 SAMUEL 2:24 NIV

In spite of his priestly duties and privileges, Eli had put his own family's interests ahead of the Lord's. It seems Eli's affections were set on the prosperity to be gained from the tabernacle offerings and on the calm to be enjoyed when his wicked sons were not provoked to anger. So he heeded his sons' rebukes more than God's.

Years before, Eli's forefather Phineas had brandished a sword to protect the nation from gross immorality (Numbers 25:1–13). Eli, however, could barely protest the open immorality and theft committed by his sons within the Lord's tabernacle. The difference between these two men was stark: Phineas acted boldly out of a deep passion for God's holiness. Eli could not rouse his behavior beyond mere lip service to the Lord.

Perhaps saddest of all is that even when Eli was confronted with the reality of his family's deep problems, he didn't seem to care. As a result, his whole family paid a terrible price.

The Bible provides examples, both good and bad, for us. Are there any issues in your family that you need to address?

Lord, please help me to act boldly out of a deep passion for Your holiness, glory, and honor.

Lord, it's sobering to think that You could nullify my life, work, and legacy in an instant if I disregard the examples of those who have gone before me.

5 TOPICS COVERED THIS WEEK:

MONDAY: the misuse of money
TUESDAY: the abuse of power
WEDNESDAY: unchecked pride
THURSDAY: illicit sexual relationships
FRIDAY: unresolved family problems

3 WAYS I THINK I'M FINISHING WELL:

1 ....

2 ....

3 ....

3 WAYS I NEED TO BE CAREFUL:

1 ....

2 ....

3 ....

How I want to respond to these truths:

....

....

....

....

....

....

....

....

LORD, HERE'S WHAT'S GOING ON IN MY LIFE RIGHT NOW. . .

OTHER THINGS I NEED TO SHARE WITH YOU, LORD. . .

Lord, when it comes to this new life map, I need to. . .

Doing wrong is like a joke to a fool, but wisdom is pleasure to a man of understanding.
PROVERBS 10:23 ESV

Thank You, Lord, for hearing my prayers and for helping me take action!
AMEN.

WEEK 27

FINISHING WELL, PART 2

A few months before his death at age ninety, Christian statesman Ted W. Engstrom invited me to Pasadena, California, to spend a day with him. Among other things, Dr. Engstrom told me about a pact that he, Billy Graham, and another close friend, Bill Bright, had made decades earlier—before they became famous. "We promised each other that we would finish well," he said. "And just think—Bill Bright did just that! Billy Graham assured me he's going to be faithful to the end. And I fully intend to do the same!"

I'll never forget his smile, the kind athletes flash after a major victory. To see the radiant face of someone near the end of life is even more moving.

J. Robert Clinton has identified five things that help people finish well. May they be seen in your life all the way to the end: (1) a lifetime perspective on living for and serving God; (2) fresh encounters with God; (3) personal daily disciplines; (4) a lifelong learning posture; and (5) lifelong mentoring by a number of people.

The time for my departure is near. I have fought the good fight, I have finished the race, I have kept the faith.

2 Timothy 4:6–7 NIV

MONDAY

SERVE GOD YOUR WHOLE LIFE

[Anna] came along just as Simeon was talking with Mary and Joseph, and she began praising God. She talked about the child to everyone who had been waiting expectantly for God to rescue Jerusalem.

LUKE 2:38 NLT

It's best to make important, lifelong decisions together, as a team, with close friends. I'm talking about the choice to live for God your whole life. This commitment can include your wife, your friends, and your fellow church members.

In Jesus' time, Simeon had God's promise that he would not die until he saw the Messiah. It seems Anna had no such guarantee, but like many others, she knew the time of the Messiah's coming was near. While these two devout people waited, they lived righteously, walking with God in obedience and worshipping Him with all their hearts.

As Mary and Joseph entered the temple with baby Jesus cradled in their arms, they looked like any other faithful couple fulfilling their duty to God. But to an old man and an old woman led by the Holy Spirit, this little family stood out like a beacon. The child and His parents were welcomed to God's house as no family had ever been greeted before.

Anna and Simeon served God their whole lives. They ended well—and with a unique blessing.

Lord, I want to serve You my whole life long. May I be as faithful as Simeon and Anna.

TUESDAY

HEART OPEN TO GOD ENCOUNTERS

When Joseph woke up, he did what the angel of the Lord had commanded him and took Mary home as his wife.
MATTHEW 1:24 NIV

Only after Jesus Christ's death and resurrection did people come to think of Him as the son of the virgin Mary. For more than thirty years He was commonly referred to as Jesus, the son of Joseph (Luke 3:23; John 1:45).

Among his many creditable behaviors, Joseph believed what the Lord revealed to him in a series of dreams—no matter how incredible those revelations were. Each time, Joseph quickly translated his belief into action, at great personal cost.

Not once does scripture record that Joseph hesitated to follow God's leading. He took to heart the reality that, "As the heavens are higher than the earth, so are my [the LORD's] ways higher than your ways and my thoughts than your thoughts" (Isaiah 55:9 NIV).

Like Joseph, you and I have a decision to make: Each day, will we choose God's will and ways, no matter the cost? Or will we decide to go our own way?

Lord, I want to experience fresh encounters with You. Please keep my heart open to You at every turn.

WEDNESDAY

DAILY DEDICATED AND DISCIPLINED

Don't let anyone look down on you because you are young, but set an example for the believers in speech, in conduct, in love, in faith and in purity.

1 Timothy 4:12 NIV

Timothy was young enough to have his ministry questioned. But he was also mature enough in his faith to be entrusted with the spiritual leadership of the church in a rather large city.

Although Timothy's father apparently was not a Christian, his Jewish mother and grandmother had saturated his young heart and mind with the holy scriptures (2 Timothy 1:5, 3:15). By the time he met Paul, Timothy was ready to convert his well-rounded biblical knowledge into active service for the Lord (Acts 16:1–4).

When Timothy was commissioned, Paul and the elders at his church laid their hands on him and publicly prophesied that the Lord had uniquely equipped him to minister to others (1 Timothy 4:14; 2 Timothy 1:6). After that, Timothy traveled with the apostle and his evangelistic team for at least a year and a half (Acts 16:1–18:19).

Not all of us enjoy a rich spiritual heritage. But like Timothy, each of us can choose today to be an example of godliness. That's good for you and everyone around you.

Lord, may I be daily dedicated and disciplined to follow You.

THURSDAY

COMMITTED TO LIFELONG LEARNING

[Apollos] began to speak boldly in the synagogue. When Priscilla and Aquila heard him, they invited him to their home and explained to him the way of God more adequately.

Acts 18:26 NIV

A hardworking, blue-collar Italian couple approached a young, eloquent Egyptian scholar. Would he care to come over for supper? Along with the meal, they served up more of what the preacher wanted most—further truth about God and His Son, Jesus Christ.

As brilliant as he was, Apollos had not yet heard the whole message of the gospel. Like someone who has read the first two books of a trilogy, he needed to learn the exciting conclusion. Priscilla and Aquila gave Apollos wonderful news: There was more to believing in Jesus as Messiah. To show one's desire to be right with God, there was more than simply following John's baptism. There was a personal acceptance of Jesus' life and work, a gaining of salvation!

Despite his impressive credentials, Apollos never assumed he knew it all. He humbled himself and his ministry grew accordingly. Apollos is a stellar example of a Christian man committed to lifelong learning. Are you?

Lord, please make me a lifelong learner.
Thank You for what I'm learning right now.

FRIDAY

MULTIPLE MENTORS FOR LIFE

The reason I left you in Crete was that you might put in order what was left unfinished and appoint elders in every town, as I directed you.

Titus 1:5 NIV

As one of the apostle Paul's coworkers, Titus must have accumulated quite a few Empire Express mileage points. Each time we read about Titus, Paul was sending him on another mission trip around the Mediterranean.

Titus actively ministered among the Corinthian believers and carried back a positive report to Paul (2 Corinthians 7:6–13). Then Titus accepted the assignment to turn around and visit them again (2 Corinthians 8:16–18). Later, Paul asked Titus to minister on the island of Crete (see above), and a short time after that, Paul directed Titus to Nicopolis (Titus 3:12).

Before all of this, Paul had taken Titus to the Jerusalem Council (Acts 15:2; Galatians 2:3). There Titus had the opportunity to be mentored not just by Paul but by Barnabas, Peter, James, and others.

No matter how much life and ministry experience we accumulate, we always benefit from mentors in our lives. Do you have a mentor right now? If not, who might you approach?

Lord, please help me to recognize and thank my mentors—past, present, and future.

Lord, I love to see the radiant smile of a man who's lived his entire life for You. May I be among their number!

5 TOPICS COVERED THIS WEEK:

MONDAY: serve God your whole life
TUESDAY: heart open to God encounters
WEDNESDAY: daily dedicated and disciplined
THURSDAY: committed to lifelong learning
FRIDAY: multiple mentors for life

3 WAYS LIVING FAITHFULLY EXCITES ME:

1 ....

2 ....

3 ....

3 WAYS LIVING FAITHFULLY CHALLENGES ME:

1 ....

2 ....

3 ....

How I want to respond to these truths:

....

....

....

....

....

....

....

....

LORD, HERE'S WHAT'S GOING ON IN MY LIFE RIGHT NOW. . .

OTHER THINGS I NEED TO SHARE WITH YOU, LORD. . .

Lord, when it comes to this new life map, I need to. . .

Listen to advice and accept discipline, and at the end you will be counted among the wise.

PROVERBS 19:20 NIV

Thank You, Lord, for hearing my prayers and for helping me take action!

AMEN.

WEEK 28

KNOWING GOD

No other question is more important than "Who is God?"
Get this one right—and experience who He is each day—and you'll enjoy life to the full. We see this truth in Deuteronomy 7:12–13, Psalm 16:2, John 10:10, James 1:17, and, well, *lots* of other places throughout the Bible.

One of my mentors told me, "When I don't take time to reflect on the God I serve, He becomes too small to help me; so I decide to handle the anxiety myself and blame God for it later." *Yikes*. Another mentor said, "I am convinced that the answers to every problem and issue of life for both time and eternity are resolved through a correct understanding of God." What hope!

I love what A. W. Tozer wrote: "The man who comes to a right belief about God is relieved of ten thousand temporal problems, for he sees at once that these have to do with matters which at the most cannot concern him for very long." Again, what hope!

So. . ."Who is God?" Five immense biblical and theological ideas stand out. We'll explore each of the five this week.

"Yours, Lord, is the greatness and the power
and the glory and the majesty and the splendor,
for everything in heaven and earth is yours."
1 Chronicles 29:11 niv

MONDAY

GOD'S AWE-INSPIRING SOVEREIGNTY

"Sovereign Lord, . . .you made the heavens and the earth and the sea, and everything in them."
ACTS 4:24 NIV

The term *sovereign* appears hundreds of times in scripture, and it's embedded more than sixty-seven hundred times in the sacred divine name YHWH. The latter typically appears as the word *LORD*—capitalized that way in most modern translations of the Old Testament.

When we think about who God is, we begin by describing Him as all-powerful (omnipotent) and present everywhere (omnipresent). Biblical heroes rejoiced over both aspects of God's sovereignty.

King David said, "The LORD has established his throne in heaven, and his kingdom rules over all" (Psalm 103:19 NIV). Paul described God as "the blessed and only Ruler, the King of kings and Lord of lords, who alone is immortal and who lives in unapproachable light, whom no one has seen or can see. To him be honor and might forever. Amen" (1 Timothy 6:15–16 NIV).

Does God's powerful presence permeate every millisecond and millimeter of your life? Yes, whether you realize it or not. You're never alone, and you're never powerless. God is with you asking, "What do you want Me to do for you?" Call out to Him today.

Lord, I thank You for Your sovereignty in my life. You are all-powerful and with me always. To know that is awe-inspiring, indeed!

TUESDAY

GOD'S PURPOSEFUL PROVIDENCE

"You gave me life and showed me kindness,
and in your providence watched over my spirit."
Job 10:12 NIV

In answering the question "Who is God?" four of this week's terms appear throughout the Bible. The word *providence*, however, does not. The term appears in the last sentence of the Declaration of Independence, and in thousands of other works published over the past 450 years. Yet during that period, *providence* doesn't appear once in the vast majority of English Bible translations. Job 10:12 in the New International Version is a rare exception.

So is God's providence an idea we bring to the Bible, or is it intrinsic to scripture? Stories about Abraham, Joseph, Ruth, David, Ezra, Esther, and other heroes of the faith clearly demonstrate God's (mostly) invisible hand at work, purposefully guiding His people and providing for their needs.

More importantly, the Lord repeatedly *declares* His purposeful providence. He assured Isaiah, "I make known the end from the beginning, from ancient times, what is still to come. I say, 'My purpose will stand, and I will do all that I please' " (Isaiah 46:10 NIV).

So does God's purposeful guidance and goodness permeate your life? Yes! Life is abundant when you recognize and rejoice in both.

Lord, I thank You for Your providence in my life.
Help me to recognize it at every turn.

WEDNESDAY

GOD'S GLORIOUS HOLINESS

*Therefore, since we have these promises, dear friends,
let us purify ourselves from everything that contaminates
body and spirit, perfecting holiness out of reverence for God.*
2 Corinthians 7:1 niv

Holy and its synonyms appear more than sixteen hundred times throughout the Bible. It quickly becomes clear that God is holy, people aren't, God expects us to be holy, and we can't be. . .without His divine transformation.

After giving the Ten Commandments to Moses, the Lord told His people, "Do not profane my holy name, for I must be acknowledged as holy" (Leviticus 22:32 niv). He also told them, "Be holy because I, the Lord your God, am holy" (Leviticus 19:2 niv).

Biblical heroes felt the dichotomies of holiness, which both challenged them and spurred their faith into action. In the middle of the Bible we're told, "Worship the Lord in the splendor of his holiness; tremble before him, all the earth" (Psalm 96:9 niv). Toward the end of the Bible we're told, "God disciplines us for our good, in order that we may share in his holiness" (Hebrews 12:10 niv).

So does God's glory and purity permeate your life? Yes! Now is the time to confess any known sins and embrace God's holiness anew.

Lord, I thank You for Your holiness in my life.
Show me the sins I need to confess, and help
me to gladly embrace Your holiness.

THURSDAY

GOD'S GRACIOUS LOVE

God's love has been poured out into our hearts through the Holy Spirit, who has been given to us.
ROMANS 5:5 NIV

Jesus and His apostles didn't "invent" the idea of God's love. Far from it.

Remember the Lord's sacred name, YHWH? Here's the first part of how God Himself defines it: "The LORD, the LORD, the compassionate and gracious God, slow to anger, abounding in love and faithfulness, maintaining love to thousands, and forgiving wickedness, rebellion and sin" (Exodus 34:5–7 NIV).

Did you notice that the word *love* appears twice in that statement?

Actually, the terms *God* and *love* appear adjacent to each other many times throughout the Bible, especially in the New Testament. The most famous of those verses is John 3:16. Other famous verses about God's love include Romans 5:5 (quoted above), Romans 5:8, and Romans 8:38–39. Still others include 1 John 4:7–10, 1 John 4:16, and 1 John 4:19.

But it's not enough to simply know *about* God's love. It is to be experienced through the time and trust we give Him.

So does God's graciousness and passion permeate your life? Yes! Open your heart to receive that divine love right now.

Lord, I thank You for Your love in my heart.
Help me to experience Your love afresh and anew today.

FRIDAY

GOD'S HEAVENLY MYSTERY

"For my thoughts are not your thoughts, neither are your ways my ways," declares the LORD.
ISAIAH 55:8 NIV

When we discuss who God is, we can't overlook the fact that He is all-knowing (omniscient). This doesn't just mean God knows all the facts in the universe. Though that's true, God knows much, much more.

Remember phone books? They contained thousands of facts, but none that could change your life. By themselves, facts are stupid. God not only possesses all knowledge, but all discernment, all insight, all understanding, all wisdom. . .and super-high-above-our-heads ways.

He Himself put it this way: "As the heavens are higher than the earth, so are my ways higher than your ways and my thoughts than your thoughts" (Isaiah 55:9 NIV).

In other words, "God alone knows," multiplied by eternity and infinity.

None of us knows a millionth of one percent of everything that's true and right and important and life changing. So why in the world are we tempted to think we know better than God? Not a chance!

Does God's higher, heavenly wisdom and way permeate your life? Yes! Humbly acknowledge His mystery today.

Lord, I'm grateful that Your mystery permeates my life. I gladly affirm that You know best how to run my life. Please do so!

Lord, I want to know You, as much as a human being can know the Creator of all. Thank You for placing delightful reminders of who You are throughout the Bible. May I never forget them!

5 TOPICS COVERED THIS WEEK:

MONDAY: God's awe-inspiring sovereignty
TUESDAY: God's purposeful providence
WEDNESDAY: God's glorious holiness
THURSDAY: God's gracious love
FRIDAY: God's heavenly mystery

3 WAYS WHO GOD IS DELIGHTS ME:

1 ……

2 ……

3 ……

3 WAYS WHO GOD IS MYSTIFIES ME:

1 ……

2 ……

3 ……

How I want to respond to these truths:

LORD, HERE'S WHAT'S GOING ON IN MY LIFE RIGHT NOW. . .

OTHER THINGS I NEED TO SHARE WITH YOU, LORD. . .

Lord, when it comes to this new life map, I need to. . .

"For Yours is the kingdom and the power and the glory forever."

MATTHEW 6:13 NKJV

Thank You, Lord, for hearing my prayers and for helping me take action!

AMEN.

SCRIPTURE INDEX

PSALMS

PROVERBS

2 TIMOTHY

TITUS

HEBREWS

JAMES

1 PETER

2 PETER

1 JOHN

REVELATION